A Walk in my Stilettos

HOW TO GET THROUGH THE STRUGGLE WITH GRACE

A Walk in
My Stilettos

HOW TO GET THROUGH THE STRUGGLE WITH GRACE

BY:

MAKINI SMITH

FOREWORD BY LINDA PROCTOR

(C) 2016 by Makini Smith.

Published by **MERAKI HOUSE PUBLISHING INC.**

For any information regarding permission contact
Makini Smith via **INFO@AWALKINMYSTILETTOS.COM**

Printed in the United States of America
First publication, 2016.

Paperback ISBN: 978-0-9949613-2-7
Ebook ISBN: 978-0-9949613-3-4
Hardcover ISBN: 978-0-9949613-4-1
Audio book ISBN: 978-0-9949613-5-8

Book cover design by
Kamar Martin

Dedication

My greatest blessings call me Mom, so it's only fitting that I dedicate this book to my princesses, Shardine' and Shakira, and my prince, Makkai. My journey truly began when they came into my world. My walk would not be the same without them, and I love them with every fiber of my being.

To my oldest sister, Andrea, whose spirit is forever with me, for holding my heart together with her angel hands, and for giving me the push to be fearless. Rest in paradise, my queen. I think of you every day!

CONTENTS

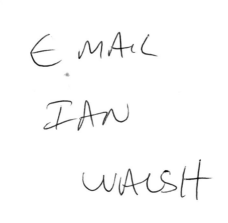

E MAIL

IAN

WALSH

Foreword

Would you like to be inspired? Well prepare yourself. The experiences you are about to encounter long before you finish this book are going to move you emotionally. As I sit thinking, and believe me, this book made me think, I have come to the conclusion that it doesn't matter who you are or what you are doing. Your age, gender, or background make no difference. You are about to benefit from the lessons the author of this book shares with you.

As your eyes travel across these pages you are going to become aware that there is something different, something very special about this book. The beautiful truths the author shares in every chapter will expand your mind. When you lay this book down and walk away, you are going to walk away a different person.

Makini Smith bares her soul. Her honesty about her life will truly impress you. This is not just another self-help book; the author is a real person. She is very much like people you know in your own family and circle of friends. Right from the opening chapter, you will relate to her and the challenges she faced.

MAKINI SMITH

Makini's life has not been easy, but with her deep faith, her courage, and her belief that there is good in every situation, she has turned every obstacle into a triumph. Oh I know, we all have obstacles and hardships, but Makini, in her young life, has had more than her share. Makini is never a victim. You never feel sorry for her. This is a story of a winner and the path she has blazed.

As I moved from page to page, I found myself eager to reach the next chapter and then the next to find out if she would actually be able to deal with these situations. I wanted to know how she would carry on and overcome. I'm certain you're going to find yourself doing exactly what I was doing: cheering her on, wanting her to succeed. AND succeed she does ... yes, she really does. By the end of the book, you will be in awe with what she has accomplished. In fact, when I finished the book, I couldn't wait to see her again and congratulate her on writing something so honest and valuable. I wanted to tell her that she had done something that would help a lot of people. And I believe that's the main point in the book: If she can do it, you know you can do it. After all, Makini is real! Her candor and the simplicity of her faith is truly motivating.

I have known Makini for only a short period of time, but I am truly impressed with her. In fact, I was impressed from the moment I met her. She has a personal magnetism that draws people to her. At our first meeting she was well-dressed and very professional. She mentions in the book that she is shy, and she does come across that way; her energy is very quiet. I think I could say that it is comfortable, but she also has an air of confidence about her.

You will find jewels in this book. These are the "take-aways" you want to highlight and incorporate into your life. I would suggest that you read this book a couple of times, focusing on how Makini dealt with her challenges and use them as a model for your own life. Invest in a couple of these books for your close friends. Put a notation on the first page suggesting they look for and take away the valuable lessons they are about to find.

- Linda Proctor
Business Woman & Author of Earn it and Enjoy It

Introduction

Loving ourselves and owning our stories isn't easy, but it very well may be one of the boldest things we will ever do. It is a process. After much soul-searching and digging deep, I've discovered how to live a full life no matter what gets thrown my way. I wear stilettos with grace. In my shoes times have been tough; I have felt pain, but I strut in confidence because with each adversity I have come through it a better, stronger, sharper person. If my head should fall, it is simply to admire my shoes! Pregnant at 17, raising four stepchildren at 22, divorced at 30, losing two loved ones to brain damage, and now a single mother—yet through it all I've overcome these adversities with a positive attitude towards life.

I have a story to tell—a story that I have kept a secret due to shame. Shame loves secrecy. It hates when we share our stories and reach out. It loves to be buried or hidden in confidentiality. I'm no longer ashamed of my story and understand that we all have a story to tell that could touch other people's lives and inspire them to carry on. So many people try to sweep their stories under a rug or bury their heads in the sand. Remove the shame, as I'm about to do with you now, and embrace the power of faith, courage, compassion, and connections. Respect your struggle and share it with those that have earned the right to hear it. I've accepted that I am not perfect and that's perfectly fine. Being real with others allows them to reciprocate and be real with me. It's a ripple effect; a gift that keeps on giving.

Now I often hear, "Oh My Gosh! Me too!"

Faith, courage, compassion, and connection are developed through practice. The ability to have and use faith to gain power in life is a skill that requires repetition to attain perfection. Faith, courage, compassion, and connection are also skills that require action and experience to learn. Like riding a bicycle or swimming, it is learned by doing. You cannot learn to ride without physically getting on the bike and riding nor can you learn to swim without swimming. It is learned through experience and consistent practice. On my journey I have learned that faith, courage, compassion, and connection are necessary tools to assist us in working our way through this journey we call life and living it to the fullest.

Overcoming adversity starts by elevating your mind. It starts by your belief that you can get through anything. It stems from having FAITH that you can and will overcome all obstacles. Be deliberate in your thoughts, paint the picture in your head, and set your intentions. For myself, much prayer and meditation on the positive outcome I desire sets the tone for me to take action and make the necessary changes in my life.

Life doesn't have to be a frustrating, never-ending experience. Like a Rubik's Cube, we are all given the right pieces and all the right colours, yet some people can't quite figure it out while others have practiced to master getting the pieces in place in no time at all. If someone were to show you how they did it, you would have the opportunity to better your odds. Overcoming adversity takes practice and a little extra effort similar to mastering a Rubik's Cube but no amount of reading or memorizing will guarantee your success unless you understand and apply.

Too often in life people talk but not about things that matter. We share photos, we share inspiring quotes, but we don't share our full stories. In fear of being judged or being the only one with that experience, we hold onto what we go through. We all have personal struggles because we are human, but we need to be deliberate in our actions. Take control of our lives. If we can't control our decisions, we can't control our lives. Through experience, I have learned that sharing experiences can heal us and help others at the same time. Every decision we make affects the direction life takes.

I have been blessed with the opportunity to share my story with the world and I'm grateful for those that have encouraged me to do so. I'm now at a point in my life where I'm prepared to give back and lay out the tools and processes that brought me to where I am today. Failure, success, romance, and tragedy contributed to my life and my walk. By understanding and applying the lessons I learned on my life's journey, I was able to reach a new frequency. I was able to stretch my self-worth to new heights and establish myself as an entrepreneur. My new level of confidence from exposing and owning my story has attracted the likes of well-known people including best-selling authors. I now work on a team with Linda Proctor, the wife of Bob Proctor himself.

This book will assist you in developing authentic relationships, building networks, and opening your eyes to opportunities all around you. Experience can be a great teacher, but other people's experiences can be even better teachers. My aim is to help you unlock what is already inside of you to reach your full potential.
Much of who I am stems from inspiration and motivation from my religious belief system, but you don't have to be of any religion to aspire for greatness and practice principles that propel you into

success. Many of today's motivational speakers rephrase the Bible to inspire and appeal to the masses.

As I take you through my journey of A Walk in My Stilettos, I want you to always keep in mind that life's rewards will not come to you due to your potential, but they will come due to your performance. You've taken the step to reading this book; now take the step of doing the actions necessary to conquer life.

"Only when we are brave enough to explore the darkness will we discover the infinite power of our light." – Brené Brown

Chapter 1

- THE POWER OF BELIEVING IN SELF -

Have faith in your abilities. Believe in yourself! It has worked for me!

Self-perception determines other's perception of you. People pick up the energy you let off. If you are insecure about yourself, others will pick up on that. They will only pick up what you are letting off. Set the tempo for who you are. That is why it is so important to believe in oneself.

I was blessed enough to grow up in a household where faith was instilled. It was shown through example as well as preached when we displayed signs of weariness. "I can do all things through Christ which strengtheneth me" (Philippians 4:13). As I got older, my mother showed more interest in the church and encouraged her children to do the same. Over time, my faith has grown tremendously. Gaining powerful faith is attained by much prayer, by reading and mentally engrossing the Bible, and by applying its teachings to my daily life.

We all know at least one person who can be considered negative. Such people are pretty much the same over the years with little to no improvement. They have a "poor me" attitude and feel the world is against them. This inferiority complex hinders all progression in their lives, but it can be overcome. By developing faith in God and believing in oneself, they can stop the unnecessary suffering and get rid of this inferiority complex.

Painting positive pictures in my head, learned from scripture in the Bible as well as reading motivational or empowering books by people like Bob Proctor have helped me to develop extraordinary faith. In the process, it gives one a humble realistic faith in oneself. For every form of adversity that can come your way, there is an answer written in the scriptures. My pastor has done an excellent job of explaining this to us in church. Whether there were thoughts of divorce or quitting a job, there is a passage that has gotten me through and shown me that I have the power to affect the outcome.

Without having a humble confidence in your own powers, you cannot be happy or succeed in life. Without faith in yourself, you are destined to fail. When you feel inadequate and inferior, those feelings will interfere with you reaching your goals, but having self-confidence will lead to self-realization and successful achievement. Having the belief that things will turn out as they should has always kept me calm in moments of chaos.

My mother was a single mother raising three of us in the home. We didn't have much money. Looking back now, things were hard, yet she displayed such strength. We were broke, but we were not poor. Poor is a mindset while broke is just not having the money for all your needs. My mother never showed signs to her children that she couldn't manage or spoke of being inferior. She believed in herself and in her provider. She worked multiple jobs, if necessary, to ensure a roof was always over our heads and that we had food to eat. In the process of her struggles, she was thanking God for giving her the strength to do so. We were rich in faith and love.

As we got older and things got harder, I noticed my mother's faith grew stronger. Her ordinary problems could be answered with ordinary prayers, but when things got tough they required her to pray deep prayers. The bigger your problems, the bigger your prayers should be. "According to your faith be it unto you" (Matthew 9:29). Prayers that are large and deep have much force and give vital and powerful faith.

My mother had a huge impact on my level of self-esteem growing up. She taught mostly by setting an example with her actions, and it spoke volumes to me. I watched her as a single mother work hard, take care of the house, dress well, display her passion for fashionable shoes, and take pride in herself and her belongings. If she wanted something she went out and got it. If she wanted a job, a car, or a house, she went out and got it regardless of what others had to say.

Believing in myself wasn't always easy. In my teenage years I was a tomboy with no shape and slender with legs that went straight up into my back, so I didn't put too much effort into my appearance. I was a fast runner, so I loved track and field but wasn't athletic enough to make the sports teams. I strived to keep my grades above 80 percent, but I wasn't the smartest kid in the class. In my eyes, I was just average. I was the girl next door that could climb trees, play soccer with the boys, and run track. I didn't feel pretty or think the boys noticed me.

On the eve of spring break when I was 14-years-old, I was with a group of girlfriends hanging out at the local mall when we were approached by two boys. I was wearing a white baseball cap, blue jeans, and sneakers. I didn't feel either of them had any interest in me, so I kept quiet as they made passes at my friends. I would let out the occasional laugh at their jokes to stay included in the conversation. After a few jokes I realized that there was laughter coming from behind me.

"Where did you come from?!" I asked the good-looking boy who was definitely the cutest of the three. He looked like he was Latin American Canadian or half-black/half-Caucasian mixed. He explained the other two were his friends. All I could do was stare. I was shy, but I thought he was super cute. By the end of the conversation I somehow ended up with his phone number. We connected and by the end of that week he became my boyfriend. That was a total confidence boost. I felt that if a guy as attractive as him saw something in me, then I must have something.

We had a great relationship and spent a lot of time together. I remained focused on my grades and did most of my homework at his apartment after school. I wasn't sure what I wanted to do with my future, but I knew that my family was proud of my grades and I wanted to maintain them so they couldn't blame the relationship as the cause of me not doing well in school.

Having just turned 17, an honour roll student, I found myself pregnant with my first child. It was a month after my birthday and there was a month left in the grade 10 school year. I was naive enough to believe the pull-out method would prevent pregnancy. I wasn't brave enough to discuss birth control pills with my mother, as her belief was I shouldn't be having sex in the first place. Purchasing condoms with the little income I earned from my part-time job at a retail store just wasn't in the budget.

The day I realized I possibly had a human inside of me, our gym class had walked to the nearby tennis court and the walk made me quite nauseous. I had attempted to play tennis and gagged multiple times. I had tried my best to act as though I wasn't about to lose my lunch until the urge was too great to hold back. I finally lost the battle and ran behind a bush just outside of the tennis court. I felt horrible. I could see stars beginning to form in my sight. I was faintish and weak. I thought to myself, "S#!@ Is this the stomach flu?"

Pregnancy wasn't the first thing that came to mind at the time. Not until the end of the school day when a series of cramps hit and had me making multiple trips to the bathroom did I decide that I needed to see a doctor. I had two schoolmates who were pregnant, so I immediately began to ask a million questions. "How did you find out?" "Was it planned?" "What symptoms did you have?"

I told my boyfriend of three years that I could possibly be pregnant, and he suggested I find out for sure. He wasn't negative or childish as most 17-year-olds could have been in this situation. He didn't have a serious personality to begin with, and I had faith that he wouldn't break up with me. At seventeen you couldn't tell me anything negative about my boyfriend. He loved me, and we were going to grow old together and live happily ever after.

I made an appointment at the local walk-in clinic and went to take a pregnancy test. I was scared, but I went alone. I didn't want anyone to know what was going on. I couldn't risk it. I hated drama and couldn't bear the thought of a rumour starting that wasn't true. "I could just have the stomach flu," I thought to myself. I knew that, regardless of the outcome, I was going to be OK.

The following day I was to call the clinic for my results. I couldn't breathe. I couldn't think straight. I felt like crap, and as much as I loved school, sitting in class was torture. I needed to know whether or not I was pregnant, and I wanted to know now. My hands were moist from sweat. I placed my quarter into the pay phone in the foyer of my high school. I dialed the number for the lab above the clinic.

"Hi. My name is Makini Smith. I'm calling to see if my test results are in," I whispered into the phone. "You will have to call your doctor. The results have been sent down already," said the technician. As I hung up the phone, I realized that it was going to cost me another quarter I didn't have. I would have to wait until after school when I got home. The rest of the day seemed like an episode of Charlie Brown. I saw faces, but all I could hear coming of their mouths was "Whomp whomp whomp."

After school, I prayed on the way home that my mother wouldn't be there when I got in. My grandmother, who lived with us in the tiny two-bedroom condominium, would for sure be home, but I wasn't concerned she would hear my call because she couldn't hear very well anyway. When I arrived home the coast was clear. My mother and her boyfriend were still at work, and my grandmother was busy in the kitchen washing dishes.

I grabbed the phone and called the clinic. "Hi. My name is Makini Smith and I'm calling for test results," I again whispered into the phone. "Pregnancy test?" the receptionist asked. "Yes," I replied. "One moment, please," she said with her sweet English accent.

As I waited, my heartbeat tried to kill me. My pulse increased by the millisecond, and the thumping in my chest felt as though it was going to jump out and land on my mother's cream-coloured carpet. I began to feel nauseous again. I repeatedly swallowed my saliva until the receptionist's voice brought me back to reality. "Positive Love," she said with her accent. "Pardon?" I asked as I jumped out of my daze. "Your results are positive. You are pregnant. You should make an appointment and come in to see your doctor as soon as possible," she repeated and hung up the phone.

Thinking, "Oh My God!" does not count as prayer. No matter how many times I repeated it in my head, I wasn't going to make it become one either. I didn't know what to feel. I lost feeling in my legs. My fingers tingled. My family was going to kill me, but I knew that I would not let it stop me from pursuing my dreams and goals in life. I had faith that regardless of the outcome, I would be successful in life because everything happens for a reason. I put my trust in God, not my circumstance.

For three months, the entire first trimester, I kept my pregnancy a secret. Other than the father of my unborn child and possibly one or two others, I said nothing. I was barely five feet tall and weighed about 115 pounds. I was petite to say the least. I concealed all signs of a growing pregnancy quite well. I got away with wearing my brother's' or boyfriend's basketball jerseys with a pair of leggings and running shoes to school every day. Fashion was flushed down the toilet along with every meal I attempted to consume.

My secret was let loose when my mother discovered prenatal pills in my backpack during exam week. I had called home from school, and the questions she asked about the contents in my bag literally made me sick to my stomach. She finally knew! I was terrified to go home. Not sure how to explain, not sure of what her reaction would be, and most definitely not ready for the backlash I was about to receive from my family, I decided to run away from home for a few days.

Straight from school I hopped on a bus to be with the father of my baby. He was happy about the pregnancy and gave me his full support. At that moment in time, in his arms is where I felt safest. From the minute I told him, he reinforced that he had my back with whatever decision I chose to make.

My mother had no idea I wasn't coming home that night. I had no bag packed and an exam the following day. A part of me wanted to hide under a rock and not even write my exam, but a part of me knew that missing my exam just because I was scared was not a valid reason and could jeopardize my future. I pushed through and showed up for my final exam the next day in my boyfriend's shirt and gym pants.

My best friend cornered me in the halls and said, "Mak! What's going on? Your mother called me looking for you. She's worried and wants you home. Please go home." But I wasn't ready. I knew she loved me, but she was rightfully upset. I knew she wanted what was best for me. I felt she would expect me to terminate the pregnancy in fear that I was going to destroy my future. At that moment, I doubted myself. It was a challenge to silence the self-doubt. Then out of nowhere a fire was lit within me. For a moment, I felt fearless.

I went back to my boyfriend's apartment where I had been hiding to tell his parents that we were expecting a child. The reaction we received was not half as bad as what I expected. His mother, a very kind-hearted timid woman, was excited she was going to get a second grandchild. His father was understandably not too pleased, so he forced me to call home and face the music. He wasn't about to be an accomplice to my act.

If I was going to prove I was grown enough to have this baby, I had to start by facing my mother. I took a deep breath and made the call. As the phone rang, I crossed my fingers that she didn't pick up. "Hello," her voice weary as she answered the phone. My heart sank. "Mom...it's me," I said as I held back tears. I informed her I was safe and where I had been staying. At the end of my call with my mother, I was instructed to hand the phone to my boyfriend's parents. I left the room to allow the adults to discuss the situation.

My mother drove to pick me up that night and have me return home. The 15-minute car ride felt like hours. In my head I imagined what she was going to do to me when we got home. To my surprise, my mother drove to my eldest sister's apartment after making a few stops in silence. The balance of that evening consisted of the lectures about being young, throwing my life away, and it being too late to terminate. It was clear that they felt not only was my unborn child's father going to leave me but also that they would have to take care of us. My mother was a single mother herself, and I could see the concern in her eyes. I knew then that I would have to prove I was not going to be another teenage pregnant girl statistic.

Over the summer, my baby's father would work full-time to save up money so we could take care of our responsibility. He would pick up baby items here and there, bit by bit. We purchased diapers, clothing, toiletries, and a stroller. By the time my second trimester began, we were well into the summer.

Only our family and closest friends knew I was expecting, so we were able to stay under the radar and prepare for our baby on the way without the distraction of gossip and ridicule. It was hard enough dealing with the comments and reaction from my family. My summer consisted of taking care of the younger children in my family—babysitting to gain experience.

We didn't expect our families to take care of the choice we made. To be honest, neither of our families was in the position to do so. My mother, working hard to pay a mortgage on a two-bedroom condo that housed five people, couldn't financially support another child. My father lived in Jamaica at the time and had about 18 children of his own to support. My boyfriend's parents, paying for a two-bedroom apartment on a single income, didn't have room in the budget for another dependent either. My child's father needed to work full-time hours to cover our expenses. Between my exhaustion and the extreme vomiting after each meal, I was unable to work.

That September was when the challenge really began. I was starting to show, and it was getting harder and harder to hide the baby bump. My high school was somehow told about my expectancy, and I was called down to the guidance office to speak with a councillor. In so many words, I was basically told it wouldn't look good to have a pregnant teen in the halls and was referred to a school for pregnant young girls.

In my mind, I had pictured being able to complete the semester with my schoolmates. I felt I could continue to hide under big sweaters and bomber jackets. Clearly I was being delusional. Pregnant people grow stomachs. I didn't want to be separated from my friends. I had never seen another pregnant teen walking the halls. I was a great student. Couldn't they make an exception? My thoughts ran rapid. I felt that if I left that rumours would start. That it would all affect me negatively somehow.

I registered for Rosalie Hall, a young parent resource centre, and realized another classmate had checked into residence. Having the option to live there or just attend the school program, I chose the latter and moved in with my boyfriend. My mother had come to terms with my pregnancy, but there was no room in our cramped condominium for a crib. I was already sharing a room with my grandmother. My boyfriend at least had his own room at his parents' apartment.

My intention was to graduate in the same time frame as my peers, so I made sure day in and day out I was in attendance. I always had a big ego and was convinced that shame would be the death of me some day. Taking the year off was not an option. That would set me back, and I knew that I would have to take some time off to be home with the new baby on arrival. I was due the beginning of February and that was enough time to finish a complete semester.

On the morning of delivery, Tuesday, January 27, 1998, it was not only one of the coldest Januarys but was also the day of a snowstorm. I woke up in pain and was struggling to walk. My boyfriend's father watched me struggle to make it to the apartment kitchen and offered me a ride to school when he saw that I was still preparing to get to class on public transit. As a true Aries, I'm stubborn, and my mind isn't easily swayed. He tried to talk me into staying home, but I refused. Pain and bad weather was not going to stop me from achieving my goals. Missing class was not something I was prepared to do. If my memory serves me correctly, we were doing final projects in class after our morning assembly, and I was determined to complete all tasks required that day.

During the morning assembly, the pain I had felt earlier that morning deepened. I always knew I had a high pain tolerance, but this was new. I had experienced false labour at seven months, so I did not feel like this was a sign that I was in labour. I sat quietly in the assembly grabbing my stomach every time the pain hit me. The girl sitting next to me could not help but ask if I was OK after observing me for some time. I politely told her I was just fine. After two more jolts of pain, she leaned over and said, "I've been counting. You're having contractions eight to ten minutes apart." I recall telling her she knew nothing because she was pregnant with her first child just like me. I waddled to class down the hall after the assembly and quietly got to work on my art project. I was determined to get through the day.

The girl that was sitting next to me in the assembly came to the class door some time later and yelled, "Are you OK?" My teacher immediately asked what was wrong and panicked the second she was told I was having contractions. I was rushed to the principal's office. Being right next door to a hospital, I was encouraged to walk next door and check-in at the emergency counter. Unfortunately for them, my stubborn ways refused. I was registered at another hospital and wanted to deliver there. My boyfriend was in his exam. I was unable to reach him, and we had paged him multiple times. I was scared, and the last thing I wanted to do was give birth in a hospital I wasn't prepared for without my child's father or my doctor.

I believe it was the principal that drove me to the hospital in the snow when they realized I wasn't going to give in. "I'm not having my baby next door," I repeated sternly. The look on my face in addition to my words made it quite clear that wasn't going to happen. I would have rather delivered right there in her office than next door at the old hospital I was born in.

I was able to leave a few panicked messages on the voicemail of my boyfriend's pager. This was obviously a time before everyone owning cell phones. By the time we arrived at the hospital he was standing there at the hospital doors waiting for me. I got my way. My hospital. My boyfriend. Once again my determination and strength to stick to what I wanted to happen worked out in my favour.

Persistence! Sticking to a plan! Making plan B is good, but knowing how to make plan A work helps get over life's ups and downs very quickly and makes the end result a reason to celebrate. The universe has a way of communicating. What you think, what you put out, and what you speak happens. Having a strong mind gives you more control of how things turn out.

I found myself giving natural birth that evening to a healthy baby girl with half of my classmates in the halls of the hospital cheering me on. My eldest sister, Andrea, was at my bedside, as usual, giving me unconditional love and support. There were parts of that evening I remember vividly and parts I don't recall. One thing I knew for sure was I was not comfortable with the idea of giving birth drugged up on medication. I had a strong belief against it and had put myself in a mental state of mind in the nine months prior that I was not going to risk the side effects to myself or my baby.

I was lying in a room filled with family and close friends, eyes closed, focused on working with the universe to have my desired outcome once more. I refused to open my eyes in fear of breaking meditation and being hit by unbearable pain that would possibly trigger the desire to scream for drugs. I concentrated on calming thoughts to sooth my mind. Positive thoughts bring positive outcomes. That was my first memory of being completely selfless. It wasn't about me or my pain. It was about the health and safety of another human being.

I believed that I could get through the labour without medication. I was sure I could handle the pain. It was a small sacrifice to make for my baby. I gave natural birth to my daughter at age 17, in a snowstorm, in the location I wanted with the people I wanted present. Some call it stubborn; I call it knowing what you want, sticking to a plan, and commanding it so. I believe in a higher being. I believe in God. I believe when you want something you work towards it and pursue it regardless of the obstacles. An obstacle is only seen as such when you take your focus off of what your goals are. Faith without work is dead.

Life is truly what you make it. Being headstrong and having faith makes anything possible. I looked like I was 12-years-old when I was 17. The world wasn't exactly the friendliest place to a tiny teen with a baby. I didn't care. I had my mind set with my goals and the only person that could stop me was ME.

Today, I am a great mother, businesswoman, philanthropist, and motivational leader. It took dedication, hard work, and persistence, but I believed in myself even when nobody else did. Never expect anyone to hand you anything in life. I put blood, sweat, and tears into the woman I am today because I believed in ME. What we think about determines who we become, and from day one I had it in my mind that I would be someone that contributes to society, someone that gives back, and would be respected.

Being a teenage mother does not mean the end of a great future. By no means am I glorifying teen pregnancy. I'm simply saying that it is possible to become a valuable addition to this world rather than a statistic on welfare. Not only do we need to believe in ourselves, but we also need to be mindful of what we absorb from those around us. Other people don't make or break you, God does. But we consume what we hear, and it feeds our minds. Every generation feeds into the next. Every generation has the responsibility to pour positively into the next. As a teen mother, I made wrong choices—I'm not perfect—but I understand we must raise a proper next generation. I took responsibility for my actions, and I've passed on the fear of God to my children so that they will make better choices than I made growing up.

What we are told as young girls affects how we feel about ourselves growing up. Teaching young girls to have ambition and high self-esteem can have a huge impact on how they turn out later on in life. Young girls are told that they can have ambition and be successful but not too much, otherwise it will threaten the male ego.

By nature, as women we have the ability to nurture, carry, and intercede. Today, I believe a woman's standards should remain high as it sets the bar for the type of people we allow into our surroundings and the quality of life we live. I keep my head, stilettos, and my standards on high always.

Through scripture I've learned that women are special to God and in the Kingdom. Our worth comes from God. To have success in life, we have to have a solid foundation. When we don't understand the importance of this, it can have a negative effect on our lives. The negative opinions of others will only affect you if you don't have a foundation and belief in yourself.

Many of us need to change our thinking. We are born royalty. Just as the royal children are trained from the time they are born that they are royalty and they are special, I was taught the same about me. Regardless of where we live or what our current circumstances or situations are, we are born royal. We don't have the ability to be paupers if we believe in ourselves.

Chapter 2

- LETTING GO AND LETTING GOD -

Fear and faith both are beliefs in the unknown—one negative, the other positive. Fear derives from abandonment, rejection, and lack of self-worth. I've observed that the people I encounter in life who live in fear remain stagnant in life. Their way becomes dark and they live an unhappy unfulfilled life. Their minds are filled with worry and failure, blocking goal-producing results. They fail to make that connection in their minds, or lack omnipotent faith, and then wonder why nothing has changed in their lives or why their prayers haven't been answered. Their pessimistic ways have robbed them of the very things they desire.

Through faith all things are possible. Faith is a bona fide power, and to the non-believer it can appear as a miracle at times. The individuals I come across that live in faith and put trust in a higher being take risks and appear to live full joyous lives. Faith requires us to think illogically because logic is like a glass ceiling. Faith based on understanding is the key to success.

Faith is not just talk. Faith is not just in your feelings. It is in your will. It requires a deep, settled persuasion and work. If I don't have something, I believe God for it and have faith he will do what he said he would do.

The intensity and persistence of my faith can take the credit for every accomplishment I've achieved thus far in life. I set goals that scare me because if I don't I become stagnant. My naysayers are still asking how I've been able to maintain my faith after my adversities and at times launch myself to another level of living.

A very close friend of mine has difficulty understanding how I'm able to sleep and take naps when situations in my life seem to be going totally unsound. When I feel I have no control over a situation, rather than drive myself insane, I say a prayer and rest my head. When you let go and let God, you're putting trust in Him that everything that is meant to happen is going to happen. I put my fate in his hands, go to sleep, and allow him to conquer my uncertain circumstances. "Cast your burden on the LORD, and he shall sustain you: he shall never suffer the righteous to be moved"(Psalms 55:22).

Back to school

I did succeed in graduating high school in the same time frame as my peers, but my priorities were not the same. While they prepared for prom, I was occupied getting babies ready for bed. While they sat in the auditorium waiting to walk across a stage and accept their diplomas, I was in line at the local grocery store buying food to cook dinner. I had to make sacrifices for my decision to bring these humans into the world.

At 21-years-old, I found myself going back to school to proceed with post-secondary education. I was a single mother of two daughters at this point. My first child was four years old and my second was five months when the relationship with my childhood sweetheart came crashing to an end. I realized that after two children, one of us had grown up and accepted responsibly while the other wasn't quite ready. I grew resentment towards someone I deeply loved when I realized his effort didn't match mine and he wasn't ready to meet me halfway. I felt total discomfort in trying to force his hand.

I was able to complete high school with honours knowing that at some point continuing to post-secondary education was in my future. I wanted to be the best me for my kids. I wanted them to have a mother they could be proud of. I didn't ever want to say to them one day, "I never continued my education because I had you at such a young age." I wanted more out of life, and I wasn't going to let the false illusion of a complete family stop me. I was depressed. I didn't feel the union of a partnership. I felt like I was taking care of the kids alone. We lived under the same roof, but he wanted no responsibility of paying those bills. I was at my wits end with his immaturity. I needed out. We were both young, yet I was mature enough to know that I wasn't giving anyone a free ride.

I had come this far through the challenges of being a teen mother and I wasn't about to fail now. My eldest sister had my back through it all. She taught me to have faith. Faith challenges your present reality. Faith reveals things and brings you to a new place. In that moment my faith in the man upstairs told me that he was going to take care of me and my girls if I put my trust in him. So I did so knowing that tough times never last; tough people do.

LETTING GO AND LETTING GOD

I had taken some time off to be a mother, but I was ready to go back to school I didn't exactly fit in with my classmates at the local college. I was in my early twenties while they were all fresh out of high school. I showed up in heels and a handbag while they had gym shoes and backpacks. They were mostly girls whose parents were paying their tuition. I was a single mother of two on OSAP (student loan). I had a mortgage to split with my sister Andrea and mouths to feed with pay from a part-time job as a data entry clerk for a worldwide shipping company. My plate was full. In my mind I had nothing in common with these girls, so I kept to myself.

There were days I would get in at the end of the day and not be able to understand just how I was able to make it through the day. I moved by faith. People that sit back and just expect things handed to them or expect God to just make things happen without them doing any physical work are in for a rude awakening. "For as the body without the spirit is dead, so faith without works is dead also" (James 2:26).

I know firsthand that God helps only those who first help themselves. We have to first have faith and believe, second do our part to put things in motion, then lastly leave it to the almighty. When we look to God as the omnipotent provider that dwells inside of every part of our being and envision it with a clear understanding in our mind, only then will he go to work and move us to where we need to be.

Being grateful and remaining positive changes your outlook; this opens up your mind and begins to manifest into your actions. God will then position you and align you with like-minded people. He will introduce you to the people that have been waiting for you to step out on faith. He will place you in situations that you can't begin to grasp or explain. Four months after ending my nine-year relationship, he brought a new man to my doorstep, literally. He was in my garage with my eldest sister's boyfriend at the time. They had come to repair her car while she was at work. He rang the doorbell asking to use the washroom. He thought my messy hair and sad, puppy dog face was cute, and I thought he was taking up too much of my energy to open the front door. I wasn't ready to date, but it was exactly what I needed at that moment.

When I think of the saying "let go and let God," I envision my thoughts and desires floating out of my head and up to the heavens. I'm releasing my thoughts and asking him to fulfill them as I move physically and carry out the actions. I read once in Bob Proctor's book You Were Born Rich that spirit has the ability to convert our present dreams into our future reality. We are requesting him to bring to life our most intimate thoughts. Personal development is our job; supernatural wonders are God's business. We just have to trust and believe it will be done.

Going back to school at this time in my life was not a walk in the park. Life was throwing tomatoes at me left, right, and center. I felt like a character in The Matrix. I had made the conscious decision to go back to school as I felt it was a needed investment in my future. Student loan wasn't enough to pay my bills, put gas in my car, and feed my babies. Working evenings after class, coming home to put kids to bed, and then studying was exhausting.

My faith was dwindling. I was worrying about things out of my control. I was trying to control everything and lost my happiness in the process. I had the love interest that had shown up on my doorstep that I wasn't embracing. I was allowing poisonous thoughts and habits to destroy my definition of love. I began to doubt my ability to continue school, I doubted if this man could possibly love me and my kids, or if I was enough. My insecurities began to expose themselves, and I grew anxious, angry, and bitter. My heart felt heavy and my life was at a standstill.

New love

In my state of pressure and confusion, the man I let in my home to use the washroom was attracted to me like a magnet. He was five years my senior, in his late twenties, had a great-paying job, and was recently separated from his children's mother. His mother was battling cancer and he was dealing with a lot in his own world, but he managed to find the time to make me feel special. Over time, we bonded over our common issues and love for our own daughters.

God can't enlarge you until you have removed all the negativity from within. He needs room to begin the makeover. The healing process starts from the inside out. I had to believe and trust that all of my hard work wasn't in vain. I had to accept that my struggles weren't for nothing. In my heart I had let go of the negative thoughts I had from the hurt of the previous relationship. I accepted the apology I never received from my daughters' father. It was then that I saw a change in my life.

I was falling, falling crazy in love with this magnificent older man. He had not met my daughters, but the love he showed for his own girls swelled my heart. At that time he made a six-figure income, which was higher than anyone's I had ever known so far. This man was so free and generous with his money that I wasn't sure at first how to receive him. He would buy us groceries, fix my vehicle, purchase clothing for my daughters, and even offer to pay my mother to watch my kids for an evening out.

I was learning to love and trust again. After being in a relationship with the same person from the time I was almost 15, I didn't think it was going to happen so soon. I had met someone that wanted to love me and my daughters, contrary to what I was told. "You think any man is going to want you with two kids at your age?" The words of my daughters' father burned my ears constantly.

This new man showed love graciously, was attentive, and was considerate of my needs. He listened and took action to win my heart. He showed me the most amount of love at a time when I felt like life was the roughest on me. He opened up my eyes to a life I never imagined. He showed me he wanted to be there for me in every way possible. I had learned to appreciate everything in my life while coming to the realization that I had asked for this but wasn't ready to receive until now.

Never ask for anything that you are not prepared to receive. God will not give you anything you are not prepared for: nothing before its time. He is the source of our supply. To the non-believer, faith may not seem realistic, but once you have it, things become very real!

Never say, "I can't" because that shows lack of faith in your mindset. Never say, "I'm not able" because that displays lack of faith in your abilities.

Never stop reaching, as reaching builds your aspirations and brings you to your desired objectives. Never stop pushing, as pushing displays your determination.

Far too many times we hear that life is complicated. Life can be challenging, but it isn't that complicated. People are. We lack the discipline and knowledge needed to succeed. "My people are destroyed for lack of knowledge" (Hosea 4:6). If we take the time to acknowledge our weaknesses and seek solutions, we can make it through. The task isn't to get over it but to get through it. Start where you are, use what you have, and do what you can with it. Make no excuses and do what needs to be done to make things happen. Not everyone will understand you, your life, and your journey. You don't require validation or approval. For me, I answer to the man upstairs. I don't require others to understand what I'm doing, why I'm doing it, or even where I'm trying to go.

Miscarriage

Approaching my second year of college I had my hands full. I was working full-time, the kids were off on summer holidays, and I had discovered I was expecting my third child (first with my new partner). I wasn't ready for more children. I was in a common-law situation with my now fiancé, but I could not bear the reaction from my family and friends. "Three kids at 23-years-old!" I could just imagine the conversations. My pride took over and I felt ashamed. I judged my situation before anyone else could. I kept it a secret and tried to cover it up just as I had done with my first pregnancy. How was I going to explain to my family that I was pregnant again? I still had one year left in school!

September came and I tried my best to act normal. My life circumstances forced me to become more of an introvert. My classmates knew me to be a quiet individual, and they had no idea what was transpiring in my world. The only person who knew I was pregnant was my fiancé. He was excited and could not understand why I wasn't as well. I felt guilty that I didn't share his joy. I was so concerned about what people would think that I allowed it to steal my joy.

I had figured out a routine by the end of September to sneak in naps, deal with the kids, do homework, and work part-time without giving off hints to others that I was expecting. My fiancé would sneak in a belly rub/kiss every chance possible. He bought me larger coats, sweaters, pants—whatever I needed. I could easily hide in my uniform smock at school. I avoided my mother like the plague, as she could sniff out a pregnancy a mile away.

I was slowly accepting that I was about to enter my second trimester with my secret baby. During a cold day in October, I was at work after class. I took a break to use the washroom and started bleeding. I was frightened, in shock, and couldn't react. I needed to leave work but had not told anyone of the pregnancy. I rushed out informing my boss that I had a family emergency, called my fiancé to meet me at home, and left. He came home to find me in the bed crying. I was still bleeding. I lay there feeling completely out of control. At that point, I knew this was in the hands of the almighty.

We drove to the hospital in silence. In my head I felt as if I were being punished for not accepting the pregnancy one hundred percent. "This is all your fault," the devils in my head persisted, refusing to be silenced.

LETTING GO AND LETTING GOD

The bleeding had not stopped, and after all the hospital tests and nurses refusing to answer my questions, I knew in my heart that I had lost the baby. The doctor finally came to explain that I had miscarried. He explained it wasn't anyone's fault and that nature would have to takes its course. "Sometimes you have to let go and let God do what he needs to do," he said.

I was sent home under orders to rest until the bleeding stops. I was devastated to say the least. I knew my fiancé wanted more children; he loved kids. At that very moment I wasn't concerned about my family being disappointed or that I was going to possibly be held back from my goals with a pregnancy once again. I felt I had called it on myself and that the universe was giving me what I deserved. I was completely guilt-ridden.

I went home and instantly began to clean everything in sight to distract my thoughts. The more I cleaned, the more cramps I felt, and the bleeding continued to flow. I was completely blaming myself, and I could not handle my own thoughts and emotions. I tried all my usual coping mechanisms to remain strong, but nothing was working. I finally had my meltdown while mopping the kitchen floor. My fiancé, who was feeling helpless watching my every move from the couch, finally came to comfort me, and I cried myself to sleep.

In my moment of weakness, I learned that the mind is a powerful thing. Thoughts become things. When we judge ourselves, we become our own worst critic and cause mental harm. There are many things in life we have absolutely no control over as things happen according to God's plan, not ours. It's OK to cry. Let it out. Allow the toxins to pour out and begin the healing process.

That wasn't easy to get over emotionally. My head wasn't functioning at full capacity after that day. I made the call to keep my baby and the miscarriage a secret, so I felt I wasn't able to confide in anyone about my loss. I was alone with God and my thoughts. I didn't know how to ask anyone else for help.

It may be easier to ask for help when you have a support system of people you trust, but at this stage in my life I felt I was being judged by everyone. I was under the impression that my family and friends had me under a microscope and that my actions were already under scrutiny. I couldn't dare give them any more reasons to pass critical judgement on my life. It can be challenging to ask for help when you don't feel you're going to get the support you need.

Asking for help doesn't make you weak; it makes you human. It shows that you want to remain strong. It's best to humble yourself and ask for the help rather than eventually be humbled when the load becomes too much for you and things begin to crumble. Learn to ask for help and not be ashamed because the guilt from dropping the ball when we are overwhelmed is harder to accept. I did damage to a friendship very dear to my heart at the time. My best friend was pregnant with her first child and expected me to throw her a baby shower as she had done for me. I didn't tell her I was hiding a pregnancy, had dealt with a recent miscarriage (I can't recall which month exactly), battling emotions, and could not handle the responsibility of her big event. I simply said I couldn't do it. She was angry with me and it caused tension in our friendship for months, if not years. All I had to do then was tell my closest friend and ask for help.

I found it difficult to come to terms with losing a baby. My emotions were in turmoil. I was overwhelmed with sorrow. Shock, depression, grief, and a sense of failure, mixed in with physical symptoms, were a lot to handle. I decided to take a week off from reality. I needed time away from school, work, and especially the demands of motherhood.

My partner and I booked a trip to the tropics to allow me the necessary space to grieve. I took my time to cope with the devastating loss but still chose to keep it between us. I had done some research and discovered that miscarriages in the first trimester are very common, and I couldn't have been the cause like I initially believed. After giving myself that time to clear my head, pray, and discuss things with my partner, I felt better. "Everything happens for a reason," my partner said, trying to console me. "That could have been God's way of removing a possible birth defect. He wants our baby to be perfect," he said as he kissed my forehead.

Who knows, maybe it just wasn't meant for me to have a child at that time? I had to accept that there are many things that I will have absolutely no control over. Let go and let God! Not everything is going to be in our control. When our plans do not align with the plans that are meant for us, life has a way of showing us. We may not approve when things don't happen our way, but the sooner we accept it, the better off we will be. Don't let the struggle take your faith; let it strengthen it. Step out on faith and let your tests be your testimony!

Chapter 3

- LOVING HARD -

We are all meant to have a fulfilled life and love hard. We were created to love; it's a basic human need. We were made with a spiritual presence that longs for connection. It's a high that some never want to come down from. It lifts us to a place of hope and fantasy. We need to trust our hearts and allow them to feel the intensity of what they want.

In my early twenties I was learning to truly love and be loved. I was madly in love with a man whose mother was dying of cancer, had four children of his own, was in the midst of a divorce, yet loved my daughters and me so deeply. As complicated as the situation sounds, I was in love with it. He opened his heart to me, and I wasn't going to ruin it. I was embracing my new life and accepting every challenge that came my way, all in the name of love. I was prepared to put in the work and do whatever it took to make us both happy. I stopped telling myself that I didn't deserve love and acknowledged that I had found someone that I wanted to grow old with.

Within the first year of being together we made the choice to live together. We couldn't bear the long hours and, at times, days of not being together. He lived in the west side of the city and I lived in the east. We were able to find a place in between from where he could commute to work and I could get to class. Compromising came with ease during this time for the both of us. He wanted me happy and vice versa. The song "Drunk in Love" comes to mind when I think back to how carefree we were. Despite his peers telling him to slow down and mine asking what I was thinking taking on an older man and four children that didn't belong to me, we were too high on cloud nine to care what people thought.

I had only met his eldest child, his son, at this point. He knew that the mother of his daughters would not approve as she knew of me and was not pleased by the gifts I would buy for her daughters. I completely understood and agreed to let him approach that in the manner he saw fit. He was introduced to my daughters only a couple months before moving in when I felt things were progressing, so I could understand as a mother the need to be comfortable with the situation.

We eventually blended our families, which was a challenge in itself. I was still adjusting to taking care of my own girls. I may have bitten off more than I could chew, but I was never one to back down from a challenge. What did I know at 22 to 23-years-old about raising six kids? NOTHING.

No one lives a perfect life. I've always believed that life doesn't give us more than we can handle. Life doesn't come with an instruction manual. We learn as we go. If we make a choice, stick with it, and move forward; we can get through it. Life is full of challenges that sharpen us and make us stronger, better people. Accepting a challenge head-on displays courage, determination, and a lack of fear. If you display confidence in your decisions, people will display confidence in you. Becoming a step-parent of four at once, I had to display strength or they were going to eat me alive. In taking on that task, I learned a few life lessons:

Be Patient

Things take time and won't happen overnight. Adjusting to a situation isn't easy. Giving it time to connect or waiting out the down times is all you can do. You can't force a situation, and trying to make it fit won't feel genuine. Time heals all things.

Pick Your Battles

Choose your battles wisely. There is no point nitpicking at the little things and making a big deal out of the things you can't control. There are going to be hurdles and landmines on the battlefield, and if you are careful you won't shoot off your own foot trying to win the war.

Be Persistent/Consistent

Quitting isn't an option. Despite possible rejection, you have to keep trying. Quitters never win and winners never quit. Most people quit right before the breakthrough. If you give up you don't get to reap the rewards and will never know what could have been.

Kill Them With Kindness

Much easier said than done, but people don't care about what you know until they know that you care. Speak love, show love, and be love. Even when you prefer to use a few choice words in a situation that isn't going well, there is no need to add fuel to the fire. Making the conscious effort to address it in a positive manner can calm the storm. Anger is the absence of happiness.

I learned very quickly to love my new partner's children like my very own as he took on the father role to my daughters. They were my new family. The chaos became normal as the kids bonded and grew fond of each other. They blended extremely well, which made things easier for me to adjust. Loving my new partner meant loving what came with him, with the exception of his dramatic ex-wife.

The world had much to say about my situation, but it was my life. Rather than try to change their views, I chose to move on without the negativity around me. In a sea of negativity, you can sink if you allow negativity inside your vessel, so it's best sailing on to a more positive path. Not everyone will like what you are doing and it's OK. Their opinions are not fact nor does it feed mouths or pay bills. I was happy focusing on my family and shutting the distractions out.

Shortly after moving in together, I took on the full-time responsibility of parenting his firstborn, eldest, and only son. I had no idea what I was getting into. It was much more inclusive than the alternate weekends and holidays I agreed to do with his daughters. All I knew was his son's mother didn't live in the country and he needed his father. They were about 15 when they had him. I was only 11 years older than him, and I knew getting him to respect me as a parent was going to be difficult.

Most men know when they date a woman with children that it is a package deal. Usually women do not have to take on that same full-time responsibility, but I embraced it. I was not going to be the cause for a young boy not to be raised by his birth father. We were barely dating one year, and my partner feared it was too soon to ask me to take on such a roll. "That's your son. He needs you. I'll help," I told him as he hung up the phone in anger. He had been arguing with his son's mother on a long-distance call.

We were already moving so quickly according to everyone else's standards. I was focused on the love this child needed and didn't give a flying pig about opinions. My mother had shown her children, through her experience of having to come to terms with the multiple children my father conceived, to accept and love children from other relationships as they didn't ask to be part of the equation. Believers in God don't need to be told when to give and never quit an assignment. With that instilled in me, I was able to convince my partner to put his role as a father first and, with my willingness to give assistance, raise his son hands-on.

His first few months involved disrespect, school principal office visits, police station phone calls, etc. I could have easily called it quits, but that wasn't in my nature. I felt God had given me an assignment, and I wasn't about to fail. This young boy was put in my care for a reason.

I was raised in government housing the first eight years of my life, and I remember it like it was yesterday. There were kids all around me with behavioural issues. I recall enough to understand that kids acting out meant there were emotional things going on inside that needed to be addressed. I chose to approach the situation in the only way I knew how: with love. He needed stability, attention, and guidance.

I was able to display to him that he was welcomed as long as he showed respect and appreciation. Things changed quickly after that. We had a few close calls when I felt like leaving and walking out on a man I loved because I couldn't handle his unruly child. We had a few moments when I questioned if it was worth staying. The poor child needed to feel love. He had been bounced around homes and didn't feel stability from his parents. "If I walked out on him too, how was that going to help?" I had to ask myself. I gave him the same attention I gave my own daughters and taught him the value of good manners. Eventually he became the sweetest child I had ever met.

Once we began to live as one big happy family, we needed a place to comfortably house all six children. We purchased a new home through a reputable builder that was large enough to accommodate eight comfortably. A beautiful 3,500 sq. ft. home with 18 ft. ceiling in the family room, step-down library, main-floor laundry, with hardwood throughout that showed like a model home north of the city away from anyone that we knew.

I was in my early twenties and most of my friends still lived at home. I was living a fairy tale life that seemed unreal to my peers, so I found myself stepping away to avoid envy and catty remarks. I was engaged, had a family the size of a sports team, owned a large home and multiple cars, and was traveling the world. I loved my life. I loved my new family. It was certainly not the life of the average lady my age.

I am love! I love hard. Those who know God love people. What can I say...It has put me in positions at times to have it bruised and battered, but it hasn't hindered me from continuing to love hard. I have tried to put boundaries on how hard I love and failed miserably. I am often loving on people who quite frankly didn't deserve the time of day. Do I regret it? No, because in the moment it felt good, it felt right, and I can't take that away. The experience didn't kill me; it hurt, but it wasn't enough to break me, so I continue. I know that my creator loves me and has given me the ability to love others. "This is my commandment, That ye love one another, as I have loved you" (John 15:12).

Not long after we moved into our new home that we purchased for the family, I discovered I was pregnant. I was terrified due to the miscarriage I previously had. My anxiety was on high. Once again, I kept it a secret. This time I wasn't concerned with what my family would think. My main concern was carrying the pregnancy to term. I didn't want to have to explain a loss if for some reason I couldn't carry to term.

I received the test results from the doctor after missing my first period and went into denial at that very moment. I refused to allow my thoughts to sabotage the outcome once again because at that time I believed I was to blame. For my entire first trimester I carried on like nothing had changed, like everything was completely normal and I wasn't with child, while missing all doctor's visits and tests in the process.

My fiancé knew my concerns and probably had the same to some degree. I was transparent about my fears and able to be vulnerable with him, completely letting down my guard. Our experience built a bond. He loved on me so hard that I forgot how scared I actually was. I was spoiled and nurtured yet confident that his support strengthened me. He reminded me that I was loved and wasn't alone.

I had carried small with my daughters, but this pregnancy refused to be kept a secret. At the end of my first trimester of this pregnancy, I was about the size of my last trimester with the girls. It required more effort to hide, and all I wanted to do was sleep. The majority of family and friends were notified when they arrived at my home the afternoon of my second daughter's birthday party. They were greeted by my huge stomach protruding out of my attire.

I was excited this time. I just wanted to see my baby come out alive. I was happy to be pregnant and happy to feel loved. I felt the timing was right, and my fiancé valued what I brought to his life. I loved and looked after his previous children, and I was going to love our baby even more. The level of love I was feeling inspired me; it ignited me. I wanted great things for our blended family.

I was ordered off of work at 25 weeks, not due to my past experience but the weight was hard on my small frame. This child wanted the world to know he was coming. I was the largest I had ever been in my life. The back pain and struggle to walk was a true test to what I thought was a high pain tolerance. I was learning my limits for pain. At times I was unable to leave the bed. My only choice (in my mind) was to bear the pain until my love child was born.

During my second trimester, my fiancé decided we had been engaged for too long and did not want our child born out of wedlock. In a matter of a few weeks he had planned our destination wedding and booked our flights before it was too late for me to travel. I was terrified of flying, and although I had flown many times before, flying pregnant was not something I was looking forward to.

When you love hard it can inspire you to take chances but can also blind you to certain things. We get caught up on the high of cloud nine and we build illusions. We paint a picture in our heads of what we want things to be and our subconscious can't tell the difference between fact and fiction. Before you know it, you're on such a delusional high, you've set yourself up for consequential disappointment.

At six months pregnant, I was in the airport heading to marry the man I felt was my prince charming—the man I trusted, gave my time and energy to, and for whom I would give my life. What happened next was clearly the universe trying to open my eyes to what was to come, but my vision was too clouded by hearts and rainbows to see.

As we sat waiting to board the plane, a group of older ladies began to discuss the fact that it was hurricane season and our destination was in the path of a tropical storm gaining strength. My fiancé saw the terror in my eyes and tried to reassure me that they wouldn't allow us to board the plane if a hurricane was expected to hit right where our plane was going to land. My nerves got the best of me and I began to shake, my hands dripping of sweat, and I had an uneasy pain in my stomach. I had a challenging time before boarding the plane to say the very least.

Once on the plane, there was a delay in taking off and I felt that was surely a sign that I should get off the plane. My fiancé reminded me that I was going to get married on a beach in a tropical island and to think of the calmness of the ocean. In my head I saw tsunamis and the water from the hurricane washing me off the beach. My fear was getting the best of me and anxiety was taking over. Under most circumstances, I would make attempts to face my fears in life; this, however, was not one of those times.

As the plane slowly moved onto the runway, I don't recall in my state of panic if it suddenly came to a halt or if it was a gradual stop. With no movement for what seemed like forever, the pilot eventually came on the microphone and announced that there seemed to be some technical difficulty and we should be in the air shortly. Really?! I am having an anxiety attack just thinking about it. At that moment I was ready to get off the plane. Getting married wasn't a concern. I just wanted to live! The tears began to flow uncontrollably. My fiancé felt I was embarrassing him and told those around us that it was my hormones from the pregnancy.

The pilot thought to be humorous after some time had passed and said, "Let's try this again shall we." Not the greatest choice of words in my opinion. To make matters worse, as the plane took off he announces, "It must have been a sticky switch, folks." All I can say is that triggered my breakfast reappearing.

If that wasn't a sign of things to come, I'm not sure what to call it. I'm known for being stubborn and doing what I want regardless of the opinions of others, but God was trying to tell me something and I wasn't listening. I was in love and about to be married.

Once we arrived in the Bahamas, the winds were heavy and the waves high. We checked in and began the final steps for our wedding the following afternoon. Sleeping that night was difficult as our room was right off of the beach, and I could hear every wave crash louder and louder. I left the bed often to observe the water come in closer and closer.

The next morning we dressed and went down to the lobby to find breakfast before our meeting with the wedding planner. As the elevator doors opened, my eyes first noticed the workmen boarding up the glass windows with sheets of wood. The hotel staff tried to assure us that this was a normal procedure as we were in a hurricane path but had nothing to worry about. My panic began to intensify, and the wedding planner had a blank look on her face as she approached us to say that the airport had been closed as a precaution and my family flying in to witness the wedding would not be able to come in.

I tried to keep it together as I walked back to my room to call my father in Jamaica. He was on his way to the airport to catch a flight to watch his baby girl get married in the Bahamas. I choked back tears as I broke the news to him that the Bahamian airport was closed because the government had issued a hurricane warning, and he should turn around before making the two-hour drive to the Montego Bay airport. I burst into tears as I hung up the phone. I just wanted my mommy.

The hotel room phone rang. It was my fiancé telling me we were going for a drive into town to get the marriage license as planned and that the wedding planner was pulling up the car. I washed my face and returned to the lobby. As I walked out to the car, the wind swept me forward. I remember thinking Hurricane Wilma was going to take my life, and I wasn't going to see my daughters again. The hormones of the pregnancy were the excuse for every public outburst of tears, and my fiancé began to take it as a joke.

That evening we returned with a notice on our door saying we would have to change rooms for our safety. They relocated us to a higher floor on the inner side of the hotel as far from the beach as possible. Moving all of our belongings from one room to the other, my mind kept saying, "Maybe you shouldn't be getting married. How many signs do you need?"

Needless to say, we got married the next day. The sun was shining, but the wind still heavy, the breeze cold, and the beaches empty. Hurricane Wilma had hit north of us pretty hard, causing over $100 million USD in damage. The hotel removed the boarded-up windows and the debris from the beach, and I got my fantasy wedding on Paradise Island. I was so blinded by love, not even a hurricane was going to stop me.

Chapter 4

- STANDING IN COURAGE -

Courage can mean many things to different people, but to me basically it is bravery—the ability to face our fears head-on. Whether it is big or small, courage allows us to be able to face our fears every day in our daily lives. From something as little as ripping off a Band-Aid to as daring as jumping out of a plane to skydive, courage enables us to face difficulty, danger, and pain without fear. The acronym F.E.A.R. (Face Everything And Rise) gets me through most of my tough times that require me to be courageous.

There is a famous quote that I often refer to when in need:

"God give me strength to accept the things I cannot change, the courage to change the things I can, and the wisdom to know the difference."

—*Unknown*

Change takes much courage because it makes us uncomfortable. It requires us to be vulnerable, and no one likes that feeling. If you are not prepared to feel uncomfortable, you will probably stay right where you are in life. In order to face our struggles, courage is a key component. Once we've walked through the struggle, it can make us feel quite heroic. When we are brave, fear can exist, but it holds no power.

It takes a certain level of confidence and says you are not afraid to make a mistake. This learned behaviour stems from experience, and given my past of having to make major decisions from a young age, I will not submit to failure.

We returned home and I gave birth to my son in a snowstorm in Toronto four months later. Things began to change drastically, and I was confused. The man I loved so hard for the last few years became a stranger. My love story didn't have the fairy tale ending that I had dreamed of.

By the time my son had turned one, my husband became a different person. Nothing was the same. The supportive man during my pregnancy was gone and I was left to deal with a colicky, breastfeeding hourly, cry every time you put him down, only wanting mommy, baby. Meanwhile, my loving partner fell in love with gambling and became verbally abusive at times. I was suffering with postpartum depression. My family was kept in the dark. I was lost and confused.

My relationship went from bad to worse. At a time when I should have been able to rely on the help of my husband, he had other things that became his priorities. He loved money and, to him, it came first. His gambling addiction worsened when he learned to play poker shortly before my son turned a year old. He would gamble online, practicing for hours on end and refusing to help with the baby or chores in the house. He would not come home some nights after spending time in casinos hours away from home. He discovered underground poker clubs within the city so he could be home before the sun came up. He would leave the country at least once per month to gamble in tournaments around the world. He was winning money, but I had lost my husband.

A relationship should be your security blanket, your safe zone. I needed my husband, but he wasn't there to comfort me. The person I felt I could depend on became undependable. I felt forced to hide my frustrations from the world and put on a mask. I had given the world the image of my perfect fairy tale blended family with this man who I loved so dearly. And now he was no longer fully invested in our relationship. It was clear to me that I wasn't in a healthy relationship, and he was no longer committed to growing what we had; what doesn't grow eventually dies.

The distance grew deeper and deeper. He no longer slept in our bed, and I could hear his snoring down the hall of our home as I sat up breastfeeding. He grew angry, controlling, verbally abusive, and hard to be around. I began to despise the person I married. I knew I had to find the courage to leave before things got worse.

As time passed, my irritation turned to anger and I allowed it to consume me. The relationship I should have walked away from was leading me. He controlled my life. He controlled who I interacted with, what I wore, and at times where I was allowed to go. I was losing control and needed help. I didn't have the courage to tell my family, and he manipulated my close friends into believing he was spoiling me; any complaint was me being ungrateful.

I lost trust, communication, and a friendship in the one person I had built my life around. They say never put all your eggs into one basket, and I felt my marriage was that basket and it had been turned upside down. All my eggs shattered on the floor with empty shells lying there, yolk running. I was afraid to leave.

I was diagnosed with anxiety disorder and mild depression but that meant nothing to my husband. One in six Canadians is affected by an anxiety disorder, so why should I get special treatment? Symptoms such as hands becoming clammy, the heart beating a little faster, even feeling lightheaded or dizzy wasn't life-threatening. Since I wasn't going to die, he made no change or effort to help improve the situation.

We tried marriage counselling, but that turned ugly. I had sensed there was more to his lack of interest in the marriage, but I couldn't prove it. I believe in picking your battles and didn't want to go to war without any weapons. I tried to fix the marriage for the sake of the kids and forgot how important it was for me to also be happy. I learned a few lessons in this situation:

Living a lie will break you. Putting up armour of denial creates pretense, and that takes a great deal of energy to maintain. The problem with living a lie is that you have to remember the lies or people catch on quickly. You may have told yourself that you are capable of living a lie. What you have not factored into the equation is the stress—physically, mentally, and spiritually—that will happen during that time.

Relationship perception becomes distorted in dysfunctional relationships. A healthy relationship encourages growth on both sides.

The dysfunctional behaviour displayed toward each other if you have children will be their pattern in love as they become adults. Your children follow mommy's and daddy's examples. They will be under the impression that your example is the norm. In some cases, the children may be too young to know what is wrong, but they will sense all is not well.

You can't live on love alone. Relationships take time, effort, and energy. Routinely saying the words "I love you" is not enough. You have to show it in your actions while your partner is around and also when they are not around. It takes sacrifice from both people, or it won't work.

It's better to be alone than in a bad relationship. Being alone and being lonely is not the same thing. Staying in a bad relationship can do more harm and be more hurtful than being single. The fear of being alone causes way too many people to stay in bad relationships, thus affecting emotional health. It takes strength to walk away but feels rewarding when you don't need a stamp of approval for your daily activities.

Staying is a form of abuse. Staying in a toxic relationship can become psychologically, verbally, physically, emotionally, or even sexually abusive—not just on the adults but it can be taken out on the defenseless children.

I was unemployed, had three children of my own, and wanted out of this eight-year relationship. I had lost my identity by his overbearing ways. I felt as though I had lost the ability to turn to my family for refuge due to my own actions. I needed a plan, and I needed to take action before things got worse. I couldn't leave without first having a source of income. I had stayed home to raise my son for four years, and getting back into the workforce was harsh during what looked like the beginning of a recession. I was halfway through a real estate course but wasn't willing to wait until that was over before putting my exit plan into place.

I had made the mistake of giving a man control over my life. We cannot serve two masters. In my moment of weakness I was attending church but wasn't present. I was numb, an empty shell, a robot being controlled by a man. The moment I hit rock bottom, I realized God had not departed. He was with me waiting for me to acknowledge him so he could give me strength. "Be of good courage, and he shall strengthen your heart, all ye that hope in the LORD" (Psalms 31:24).

I made the courageous decision to end my marriage almost five years after it began. I was willing to risk so much for the unknown. I made myself vulnerable to criticism, loss of lifestyle, loss of family/friends, and life as I had known it.

God took the driver's seat of my life and gave me the strength needed to leave. I felt heroic in every step I took towards my freedom. I felt powerful standing up to someone that once made me fear for my life. Don't get me wrong, I had fear, but I pushed past it. Courage is the ability to face adversity and overcome it DESPITE your fears. I operate on ridiculous levels of faith, and that alone gives me the courage to make decisions others would be too afraid to make.

When I made the choice to walk away from my marriage I had no idea that meant I was going to lose everything I felt I had worked so hard to build. The relationships with four stepchildren ...lost. My financially stable lifestyle...lost. My best friends...lost. My family's perception of my happy home...lost. I was at ground zero. I suffered an ugly divorce, to put it mildly. Not that I believe there is ever a pretty one. Yet again, I had felt like I had become the statistic I was trying so hard not to be.

He surprised me every step of the way with how low he would go. It went from a battle for support payments to the kids no longer being allowed to communicate under his orders. Each argument would top the last. It was a new level of hurt and surprise I was left feeling about the stranger I was battling. The man that had loved my daughters and me so hard was now so cold and heartless towards us. He had washed his hands of the little girls he had raised for almost nine years. I had to remind myself that it wasn't me; I wasn't the villain for wanting out. Having the courage to leave would one day have its rewards.

I have to admit the greatest hurt was watching it have an effect on my girls, which took a strain on my mental powers. My son was only four years old and easily adjusted to seeing his dad on weekends. My first heartbreaking moment for the kids was when my eldest daughter realized all her step-siblings had deleted her from social media. The kids had nothing to do with it. She had no idea why she was being punished. The second heartbreaking moment for them was when he called from his vacation with the new girlfriend to speak to my son and didn't acknowledge my daughter that had answered the phone, not even asking how she was doing! Both incidents in the same week, four months after he had moved out.

How do you explain to children that the man that acted as your daddy for over eight years no longer acknowledges your existence and it has nothing to do with you?

The devastating part was trying to remain sane during all of this when a bomb was dropped in my lap. I was sitting in church one Sunday and received a text message from a random phone number: "Good thing you left him. He slept with your best friend and he tried to sleep with me too. So nasty."

I was sitting between my eldest sister and another woman, and it was as if the entire church had disappeared around me. I couldn't hear anything, see anything; all my senses had left me. I went numb. Thoughts ran through my mind of how that could even be possible. "Who is this?" I replied to the message.

As I waited for the answer, I prayed it was a horrible prank. I thought about my present environment and realized that there was a reason that message came while I was in church. If I had been anywhere else I would have committed a crime. As my pastors voiced chimed into my ears, the congregation began to clap. My sister looked at me and asked, "Are you OK?"

I looked at her and nodded because words could not come out. The phone vibrated in my hand. The answer was nothing like what I expected. It was clearly someone that knew details of my life. They proceeded to tell me that the trip my ex had paid for my girlfriends and I to celebrate my birthday in Las Vegas with him was one of the times he had slept with her. They knew of the one night I went back to the room alone to sleep because I was exhausted.

I became a zombie after that text message conversation. The following day, I sent the kids off to school and thought I'd stay home and clean to gather my thoughts. I brought a load of laundry up to my son's room after seeing the kids off to school. I sat on the edge of his bed and my mind began to race. I knew I had lost track of time sitting there, but when I heard the front door close and the kids' voices at the front door, I realized I had sat there ALL day in a daze.

The kids returned from school and I was sitting in the exact same spot on my son's bed from the time they left that morning. I felt I had lost my sanity. I said nothing to anyone about what I was told for days, not until I got the nerve to tell my sister because I needed her resources in the telephone industry to trace the cell phone number. What was this person trying to do? Why did this person feel the need to share this after I had already left him?

After coming to a dead end with the phone number once we discovered it was a pay-as-you-go with no real name to attach it to, I decided to further my research. Growing up, my mother always said, "Whatever it is that you are looking for, you will soon find it." And find it, I did.

I was cleaning out a drawer and came across one of his phone bills that he had set aside to reference when he had called the phone company to dispute some of the charges. I spotted my so-called best friend's number more than once. I grabbed a highlighter and marked every call. The rage grew with each line I crossed out. I was beginning to overheat.

How could she do this to me? I loved her like a sister. I shared everything with her, but my husband should be an exception. I contemplated how I would confront her. I decided I would allow her a few minutes to explain before I got physical. I played out in my mind how I was going to run her over with my car. I envisioned how I would get him there to watch. I was livid.

My sister was able to rationalize my thoughts, playing on my love for my kids. "You can't go to jail. What if they grant him custody?" she asked me. She was correct. I needed to calm down before I did something drastic. She prayed with me and we talked. I knew my anger wasn't going to amount to anything productive.

I wanted answers. So I did more research. I was done with the marriage, but I was hoping this was all a misunderstanding and I could save the friendship that I looked at like family. I mustered up the courage to confront my ex about what I had learned. As expected, he laughed and called me crazy. He had no logical explanation for the evidence that pointed against him.

I was beginning to feel like a fool but refused to let it go until it was proven true or false. I made arrangements to meet my so-called "bestie" in a public place to hear what she had to say face-to-face. Arranging to meet in a restaurant was my only saving grace. It was filled with enough people to prevent me from embarrassing myself (I loathe embarrassment) with any act or behaviour that could occur from such a situation.

I have to say I was pretty proud of how I handled myself that evening. I maintained my composure, and my temper, with grace. As she shed tears and explained how much I meant to her and she would never do such a thing to betray me, I felt compelled to believe her. What can I say ,I have a big heart.. I was naive.

For weeks, she and I made efforts to mend the strained friendship. I believed she had the best interest of my kids and me at heart. I had always been there for her. I couldn't have been more wrong about her.

More and more people began to confess to me that they had something going on. Some called it old news while others said they didn't have the heart to tell me while I was still with him in case I didn't believe them. I felt like a fool. I felt like everyone knew except me and I was the laughing stock of our circles.

Her true colors showed shortly after when I filed for the divorce. I asked for her assistance in confirming the series of events that happened on a particular day when she was present that would have a major effect on the outcome of my divorce. After she had agreed, she reneged and was furious that I would involve her in a situation she had involved herself in to begin with. The letter she decided to send to my lawyer was filled with falsification. Clearly asking her to tell the truth was too much.

I decided then to cut my ties on the friendship and let go. I had given her a chance to redeem herself and I felt she let me down. I know that God doesn't sleep, and if she was guilty of sleeping with him, she would one day reap the harvest she had sown. My eldest sister had given me many talks and much prayer, and I was angry but realized that doing nothing about it didn't make me weak or a loser.

Having the ability to say nothing or do nothing takes great strength and courage. It takes superhuman strength, depending on the situation. Being able to leave things to karma requires special power also. Most people could not have left the situation and walked away so easily. I'm human—sure at the beginning stage I thought of revenge plots, but what kind of person would that make me? I would be just as bad as her if I chose to find ways to get back and hurt her. My morals and the way I was raised may have something to do with it, but I don't look at it as a weakness. I know it takes tremendous strength. Picking your battles wisely is a trait I hold with honour.

I have to thank God for the support system that was there for me during that time. My eldest sister had always been there for me, and this time was no exception. She was a strong praying God-fearing woman. She had moved in with me during the first six months of the separation and spent many nights helping me comfort the tears of two broken-hearted little girls. I couldn't understand his actions and made it a point not to because I felt the moment I could justify his madness that meant that I too had gone mad.

My kids and I had to adjust to a complete lifestyle change. I had moves to make and had to make them fast. I had come from having little and could manage if I had to temporarily go back to that, but my kids had no idea what it was like to have a need and not have it met. Some would call it spoiled, but I say they were blessed in many ways, aside from the material things, and pulling the rug from under their feet would have been a hard reality check at that time. They were hurting enough. I was determined not to be a failure in their eyes, and playing the victim wasn't my style.

I had to complete my real estate course and make it work because a nine to five at minimum wage wasn't going to feed four mouths, pay the mortgage, cover the divorce lawyer, and maintain my vehicle. Plan B was figuring out how to make plan A work!

Divorce lawyers are not cheap; maybe I should have gone into that field to maintain my lifestyle. At today's divorce rate of $350 per hour, I'd be pretty comfortable. Being billed for each e-mail, each phone call, and paying thousands of dollars for each court appearance that led nowhere, hurt when I know that money could have gone to benefit my children. I was being taken to the bank by both the lawyer and my son's father. His tactic was to drag it out until I ran out of money because his supply seemed to have no end and mine was near.

Growing up, I had always heard the saying, "God doesn't sleep; he sees all." For every challenge in the divorce period these words gave me the ability to prevail. I strongly believe in karma. My ex-husband's negative actions would, according to cosmic principle, be punished if not today some day in the future. God would not sit back and allow him to hurt these children and get away with it. He would repent at some point.

Relationships can feel so good yet hurt so bad once they come to an end. As humans we are biologically, physically, and spiritually wired to love, be loved, and belong. When a relationship fails, we don't function as we normally would. I was hurting but I had to be strong for my kids.

The divorce was the moment I gave reality to the fact that I had to pursue real estate full-time as a career. I was officially self-employed with no security blanket or backup plan. When you have a business to run as an entrepreneur, the consequences can be more severe if the effort put into the business is lost as we grieve. My business couldn't afford emotional days off.

I was at the start of my real estate career and the height of my divorce all at the same time. I had three little mouths to feed and the cost of letting the breakup affect my business was much greater than I was willing to pay. I had to make some courageous choices and make them fast. I didn't have time to wallow in self-pity. There are no paid vacation days or any other form of magic money to pay the bills and feed the family should I choose to sit in my room and cry about the loss of my husband.

Within the first year of the separation, I had racked up a $20,000 lawyer bill and was $30,000 in credit card debt trying to survive and get started as a realtor. I had never seen a debt higher than a few hundred dollars before and wasn't even sure how I got there. I felt it was my issue to deal with, so I didn't exactly know how to ask for help and I wasn't about to let him win. I was angry. I was angry with him and most of all angry with myself for letting it get to me so much.

We always have a choice in life. I chose to be an entrepreneur when I became a single mother, so I knew that came with sacrifice. Entrepreneurs already have a mindset that separates them from the nine-to-fiver (someone that works to build someone else's dream). Drive, motivation, and passion is what ignites the fire to succeed. Going through my divorce just added fuel to that fire. Not only did I want to come out of the divorce on top, but I also wanted to succeed in business too. And in order to make it work I had to have my mindset in a place that had the courage of a lion.

It was time to focus and get my s#!@ together. The three main approaches to dealing with anger are expressing, suppressing, and calming. I let the anger out and expressed my feelings verbally. I suppressed my anger but attended to the grief while working on adding to my business. Calming the anger took work, but I found comfort in the gym to let out my frustration. Once my anger was redirected and the energy focused on bettering myself and my business, it paid off.

I was determined to win, and win I did. I used every one of his attempts to get under my skin as fuel to do that much better for my kids and myself. I refocused that energy into my business and hit award levels, made top producer in my office, and paid off all debt in that year. I stopped allowing him to have control over me and my emotions. Every time I felt I was backsliding and my business was feeling the effects, I shut out the distractions of the breakup. I wouldn't answer his calls, read his texts, or engage in conversation that involved his name. Not communicating was essential to healing and relieving distractions.

As much as I loved him, I loved myself more. I wasn't about to let him take my heart as well as my business with him. I knew it couldn't rain forever, and if I could maintain keeping the ship together long enough, I wouldn't sink. God was equipping me for something. My suffering was not in vain.

Sometimes we confuse the tests in our lives with weight. The struggle is our training. The test is designed to develop you, sharpen your skills. We learn best through experience in life. The take-away lessons help us grow if we acknowledge what we are meant to learn from them. If we fail to learn the lessons, life will repeat those experiences until we learn what was meant to be learned. In other words, until we finally get the picture. "I will instruct you and teach you in the way you should go; I will counsel you with my eye upon you" (Psalm 32:8).

Making challenging decisions is pertinent to our success in life. Great thinkers are all decision-makers and that comes with experience. Our circumstances can change the second we decide to make a choice. I chose to end a marriage. I knew my life would change but not to what degree. It didn't matter at the time. I wanted change and I was prepared to be uncomfortable in order to make it happen. Have you ever thought about how much your life could change if you had the courage to make life-changing choices?

Courage doesn't have to be loud; it can be that small inner voice giving you the strength to carry on. Conquering life one struggle at a time is still powerful. My moments of courage came to me at night when I could say to myself, "You got through today. Tomorrow is a new day," or the mornings when I had to pep talk myself out of bed with, "Today is your second chance. You can do this." Scripture has taught me to be strong and courageous; to not fear or be discouraged because God is with me always.

Chapter 5

- STARTING OVER -

Today is the first day of the rest of our lives. We are entitled to rewrite the script for tomorrow's show. The pictures that we paint in our heads for tomorrow can be changed the second we change the way we look at it. When we decide to take those steps to start over, it is important to keep our ears open only to people who truly support our desire for change and growth. When life calls for change, we have the choice to go backwards, be stagnant, or move ahead. The environment we surround ourselves with in that moment will determine what path we take.

We are all deserving of new beginnings. I needed a fresh start, a clean slate, newness. I was ready to move ahead and start fresh, but I had no idea what to do, where to go, or how to get there. Most successful people set a goal and have no idea how they will get there until they actually reach the goal, but they understand that their thoughts affect their outcome. It's all about intention. I had been an aesthetician, I had been a stay-at-home mom, and was now a real estate agent. It was time to make some more changes. I needed to focus on my goal and make it happen. I surrounded myself with those I felt honestly supported me and began my quest for change.

I made an effort to stop believing in why things could not be done. I gave all my energy into succeeding. Your mind is what drives your actions. What we believe is what we become. Wherever we focus our energy, that is what manifests in our lives. It was a habit I had to practice. Belief is a learned behaviour. "Trust in the Lord with all of your heart. Lean not on your own understanding, in all your ways acknowledge him, and he will direct your path" (Proverbs 3:5-6).

Nothing that you need is outside of you. You have a deposit of wealth in you and God's light shines through. "Let your light so shine before men, that they may see your good works, and glorify your Father which is in heaven" (Matthew 5:16). Starting over or moving forward requires persistence and dedication to succeed. That is all inside of you.

We are conditioned by habit. All people are hardwired to do what they have been doing to get the results they are getting. This creates struggle to change. To get a dramatic change in our results, we must first discover what we want. Thinking about the results creates a distraction, but when we think about the goal of achieving what we want, it motivates us. We are motivated by our wants.

Situations and distractions are bound to come along, but they are only meant to deter you. They come for a reason. Distractions come to throw you off and make you think you are doing something wrong and, in some cases, make you feel you are achieving something when you are really not. Don't allow your circumstances to deter your goals.

Your current situation doesn't define you. Moving forward and starting over if needed is your breakthrough. Many are permanently stressed out and unpack their life in one spot due to a negative situation because they don't understand trouble. When we go through the test, we can then share with others our testimonies to inspire and uplift them.

To some, I had a delusional perception that I would do well when my current situation seemed to be working against the odds. I was a single mother with three dependents, a mortgage to pay, an SUV to maintain, an introvert personality, and next to little savings. Those around me had much praise for my drive to start fresh, but in the same breath stated why they could never do what I was doing. I found myself tuning out of conversations that made me doubt my ability. I couldn't engage in the negative energy. They didn't have it figured out, so why would I absorb their opinion about a life that they knew nothing about? Why would I allow small minds to tell me my dreams are too big?

I was on a new path, and I wanted to be different. I looked at my situation and realized how unique I was and how strong I had to be to endure my past and still have the desire to succeed and keep pushing when others would have given up. The self-help books I had been reading and the positive people I surrounded myself with made a significant impact on my life. We are a product of the books we read and the people with which we surround ourselves.

I had to step back from some of the people I called my friends. Both success and failure hinges on associations. I had to take a chance and get to know new people of like mind. I stuck my ego in my back pocket and reached out to heavy hitters via social media. I wanted to learn good habits from positive, successful people. Energy is transferable, and I wanted to learn to be a better person. Personal development is our job, but supernatural wonders are God's business. If I were supposed to benefit, he would make it happen.

I had spent years following orders and being told what to do. I wanted to be around others yet not follow the crowd. I wanted to be mentored but not influenced into making decisions based on the opinions of others. It's natural to want to follow the crowd as we don't want to feel like the odd ball out, but if I had learned anything from the controlling marriage it was that following others was destructive.

I took about a year to observe and learn from those I was surrounding myself with before I noticed a change in my life. From colleagues to friends, I was taking in and trying to understand their habits both good and bad. Taking away the positive to form the new me and filing the negatives as the things I wanted nothing to be. I was gaining understanding from others, as I could not do it solely on my own. "Whoever trusts in his own mind is a fool, but he who walks in wisdom will be delivered" (Proverbs 16:18).

That year had much to contribute to the transformation of the new me. I picked up some nuggets that have improved my life.

1. **Passion** – If you're going to succeed at anything, you must first love it. If you don't enjoy doing it, there is no fire lit inside of you to keep you motivated.

2. **Work** – If you're not willing to put in the work then you don't deserve it. The reason why most people that win the lottery go broke shortly after is because they didn't earn it.

3. **Focus** – Keeping your eye on the prize and not allowing distractions to sidetrack you will get you to the end goal faster. Don't pay attention to what others are doing unless it is connected to getting you closer to your desired result.

4. **P.U.S.H.** – Pray Until Something Happens. I am who God says I am, and he will make things work for the greater good. You have to want it and be willing to be consistent. Push yourself and know you are not alone. Believe in a higher power.

5. **Ideas** – What makes you different from everyone else trying to do the same thing? You don't have to reinvent the wheel, but you need to have ideas that make you stand out from the crowd. Find your edge and push past it.

6. **Improvement** – Each day is your opportunity to be better than you were the day before. Constantly look for ways to improve yourself as well as your work.

7. **Service** – The universe has a way of reciprocating what we give out. Serving others gives us power, joy, and wealth of all forms. Service given with an open heart and an open mind does not go unnoticed and spreads like a wildfire. Be of service. Money is a reward for service rendered.

8. **Value** – No matter where you go or what you do, add value. Align your core values with how you offer value to create stronger relationships and build wealth in finance, love, and relationships.

9. **Delegation** - We are only given 24 hours each day. In order to live full lives, it is more effective to do what we do best and to outsource tasks that we're not good at to people who excel at them. Don't try to be a "jack of all trades and master of none."

10. **Persistence** – You need firm continuance in a course of action in spite of difficulty or opposition. There will be hurdles and potholes along the way, but you need to get over them quickly to reach your goal. Persist and develop the courage to move on, even when everyone around you is telling you it is OK to give up.

It took some time (eight months to be exact) before I received my first paycheck as a reward for my efforts, but the taps had opened up and the paychecks began to flow after that. Money is a reward for service. I had definitely earned it for the level of service I was providing. I had never earned that kind of money on my own.

I was forced to make many changes in myself to adjust to the real estate world in order to make a living. I was forced to realize that my mindset held much more weight than I had given credit. I discovered I was able to achieve more just by having faith, being proactive, and seizing every opportunity.

I was a very private person before I became a realtor. I had to learn to open up and have conversations with strangers. Real estate is a relationship business, and when you are selling a service verses a product, people won't work with you if they don't feel they can relate to you. I had to learn what it is to be an entrepreneur.

I had to open up to the idea of sharing who I was in order to build real relationships with not just potential clients but also with the people that existed around me in order for them to feel comfortable referring my services to their friends and family. Being open about going through a divorce and being a single parent was hard enough on its own, but I found being transparent about my life made me relatable—a human being that had needs and desires just as they did, not just someone out to make money off of them.

I had to learn to network. I was accustomed to being the fly on the wall and finding a corner to sit in when I entered a room so no one would stare at me or try to make small talk. Your net worth is determined by your network. It's a numbers game. The more conversations you have, the closer you are to your next deal. Small talk has never been easy for me, but starting with complimenting someone has never failed.

I had to be skilled in branding myself—marketing myself online as well as print, the message I wanted to deliver, and living out my brand in my actions. You have to be consistent in your words and actions. You can't expect people to take advice from you or use your services if you're portraying the opposite in your way of living. If I promote that I give quality service and my marketing looks very poor in quality, that's not good marketing.

I learned that every opportunity is a lesson and learning from an experienced person in the business can give you the tools you need, but it's up to you to build on your own. I've been fortunate enough to be able to learn from some really great realtors. They have been very generous in sharing tips to help me develop my skills, but not everything works for everyone. My takeaways are the tips that I feel will benefit others.

One thing I learned is that there is strength in silence. There isn't always the need for a verbal reply, and sometimes saying nothing doesn't mean you lost the battle but that it isn't worth fighting. Perception of a situation can be very different for each person involved. Investing energy into trying to change a person's mind if they are convinced they know everything is a waste of time and energy. I've won many battles by just staying quiet and allowing things to be.

I also had to digest that a book is always judged by its cover, even when they tell you that it isn't. From the minute I walk into a room, I'm being judged. If someone doesn't like the way you look, it doesn't matter what comes out of your mouth after that. Your outfit doesn't have to be expensive, but you need to be well put together. Your attire needs to match your profession to present and air credibility. I've seen realtors meet clients in jeans and sneakers or summer shorts and flip-flops and I didn't take them seriously. Your appearance matters, and it's better to be over-dressed and polished when it comes to business.

I also grasped that helping others along the way has much more rewards for your life and business than just financial. Reciprocity goes a long way. Sharing knowledge and resources, and being generous and genuine, has helped me build relationships with many influential business professionals.

I am forever a student of life. I strive to grow daily to become a better person. I was being taught lessons daily. The more I learn, the more I adapt to the changes around me. It's not the strongest or most intelligent that survive, it's the most responsive to change. As things changed in my personal life drastically, the world outside changed also. I've become accustomed to embracing change and expecting it in order to grow.

I was never a fan of the traditional nine-to-five idea, being paid by someone else to build their dreams, and working to death for someone else to tell you when you can take a vacation. Feeling guilty when you have to leave to pick up a sick child from daycare wasn't my idea of a dream job. Making the choice to be an entrepreneur and build my own dreams on my own terms has been much trial and error, but at the end of the day all decisions are mine to make. I am my own boss. I control whom I work with and when I work, and at the end of the day, whether I win or lose, it's based on me. Making it your goal to reach your full potential helps attain spiritual fulfillment, emotional health, and mental satisfaction in life.

Regardless of the outcome of my efforts, I gained experience. Failure is not an option, only a lesson. Even when things didn't go exactly as I planned, they happened as they should. Things happen according to God's plan, not ours. So the timing may be off or it may not happen precisely how we envisioned, but it happened exactly as it was suppose to. Every lesson is a blessing. We've been conditioned to look at failure negatively. The most successful people in the world understand that each failure is a step closer to their success.

In my journey of transformation, I've taken many risks. I didn't have the security blanket or the luxury of a comfort zone. I was open to taking risks to win big. As much as I despised the gambling habit of my ex-husband, I realized how big you can win when you take a chance. I found a positive way to look at it. Risk is equivalent to faith.

Chapter 6

- FRIENDSHIPS-REASON, SEASON, OR A LIFETIME -

I'm a firm believer in people coming into your life for a reason, season, or lifetime. During my life I've met some amazing and some not-so-amazing people. Some I've met and learned valuable life lessons from while others have made me experience blessings. We make connections with people every day. From the teller at the bank to a neighbour on your street, the connection you make can be superficial or end up being a lifelong bond. It's a part of life.

When those connections break we feel discomfort. Most of us have taken a chance getting to know someone and feel disappointed when the relationship falls short of our expectations. Some of us even dwell on the loss of invested time and effort. If we understand that each interaction has a significant meaning in our lives, we can then understand the value in every connection, no longer viewing each as a loss but an experience.

There will always be people you had to meet for a reason. It could be simply to learn a life lesson or perhaps they are the connections to your next level in life. Like taking a connecting flight to reach the amazing destination you so look forward to. I have met people I feel whose sole purpose for being in my life, at a point in time, was so that I could meet another person in their circles. Every connection has a purpose. Not every person you meet is meant to stay in your life forever, and the sooner we accept that, the happier we will be. I don't hoarder people around me because I am able to recognize that holding onto people that are not meant for you prevents you from moving forward. They block your blessings and you become stuck in a stagnant place and are left wondering why.

Some came in quick like a freight train, making so much noise, and I had no idea what was happening. They showed me a world of fun and much love then hurt me so unexpectedly that I had to accept that they were just there for the season and the lesson I needed to learn at that moment in time. I am blessed with a handful that I call my foundation. These are my lifetime friends that have been around since before I had children and are always there for me. They kept me in good spirits through the divorce and supported my decision to be a realtor. They have kept me on my positive mentality path and strengthen me regularly with their support.

I'm an introvert so I don't enjoy small talk, struggle with large groups, and prefer quality connections. Many people are and don't even realize it. Given the choice, you'll devote your social energy to the people you care about most, preferring a glass of wine with a close friend to a party full of strangers. You think before you speak and have a pleasurable appreciation for seclusion. You feel energized when focusing deeply on a subject or activity that really interests you. You have an active inner life and are at your best when you tap into its abundance.

One day, I made a connection via social media with another realtor. I had found that the easiest way to make quick connections. She and I had never spoken on the phone, met for coffee, or been face-to-face for that matter. I was drawn to connect to her because of her positive posts that had inspirational quotes. One day she invited me to a women's networking event because she had no one to attend with her. I was in a mental place where I was challenging my own abilities to be social, which, after a few days of consideration, provoked me to accept her invitation.

I arrived at the event and we introduced ourselves before going in. Once inside, we made small talk about real estate and things of that nature. I'm an introvert and not very good at small talk, so I did my best to answer her questions with answers other than "yes" and "no." I smiled during the conversation and seemed to attract the attention of other women in the room. As others came over to introduce themselves I smiled and handed them my business card.

As the event started we were all separated to numbered tables to force us to network outside of our comfort zones. For the rest of the afternoon I was alone at a table with women I had never seen before in my life. A part of me wanted to leave and the other accepted the challenge of making the most out of it.

The event was to be three hours long, and I had made plans for immediately after. When I realized that it could possibly be an hour more than expected, I texted the lady who had invited me to inform her I was leaving and that we would connect again soon.

I have never seen her again, but her invitation changed my life in more ways than one. She is someone I can say I met for a reason. We had pleasant conversation that day and have had a few short text conversations since then, but neither of us made any effort to build that relationship.

Had she not invited me to this event I wouldn't have made a sizable donation to the cause of child sexual abuse, I wouldn't have met the organizer of the event and would have missed out on the friendship I have built with her. I wouldn't have had a reputable guest speaker for my very first fundraiser that I put on to support a foundation for children in my community and donated all proceeds to the charity. I wouldn't have graduated and gone on to be a leader for a women's group called Sister Talk created by Karlyn Percil, which was featured on the Oprah Winfrey Network multiple times. It's a unique platform where women meet monthly to have real and honest conversations about life, love, careers, and relationships through open dialogue and tackle the things that prevent them from reaching their goals.

Becoming a realtor and being required to come out of my turtle-like personality of being an introvert, I have had to network and meet many people. Accepting that many of those people are simply for a reason helps me keep my emotions in check when we don't stay connected. They don't want to do business with me. They don't want to be my new best friend. We exchange contact information knowing that we may never speak again or only connect again should a reason come up.

Since becoming a socialite, I am now out regularly at networking events or consistently a part of networking groups. I am there to connect with people in hopes of not only finding a lead to that next deal but in hopes of finding that next clue or the key to unlock the next level of life. All the keys in life are given to us; it's up to us to recognize them and to make use of them. Opportunities are right in front of us all the time. The sooner we learn to sight the opportunities, the more successful we become. We all have the same 24 hours in a day, so why is it that some people are super-successful and others struggle once put in the same situation? Recognize the tools/people that are given to us. I don't believe it is using people if your intentions are good and your heart is clean. It's recognizing their reason that God connected you to them in the first place.

Seasonal people that you encounter come to get you through a place in your life that you may not have been able to get through on your own. There was something in your life that you were experiencing and needed a change. They came to teach you something. Seasonal people can be around for a long time and can be disguised as a friend that you feel will be there for life. They become a large part of your day-to-day and before you know it, it's over. You're left answering questions like, "What ever happen to so and so?"

After getting into real estate, I had opened up myself to many new people. Doing so opened the door for a lot of great connections but, at the same time, a lot of hurt. I was pretty good at weeding out the people I call "Reasons." My weakness was identifying the "Seasons" people, and we don't usually recognize them until the seasons change.

I had gone through my experiences with the divorce, my ex-husband's betrayal, and my hurt from my closest friends, so I had issues being close to people. It was time to stop hurting and time to start healing. I opened up my heart to a few women that I felt I meshed well with. They were loving, fun, exciting, and open to adventure. I was at a point in my life where everything about them appealed to me and I welcomed their friendship the more I got to know them.

My divorce was official and I wanted to celebrate everything life had to offer. The newfound friendships brought an entire different meaning to the word celebration for me. Every day was a reason to celebrate, and surrounded by my new friends we did just that. Weekends, after work, we would get together. Once a week, on a weeknight, we gathered as a group to celebrate our highlight of the week. Together we celebrated birthdays, real estate deals, and everyday minor accomplishments. They had brought joy into my life at a time when I needed it most.

They taught me to celebrate the little things, the big things, and everything in between. They had showed me that even though I had been hurt and betrayed I was still capable of once again experiencing loving friendships that brought pure joy. I appreciated every moment we celebrated and was grateful that I was being shown that I wasn't bitter from my past experiences and could feel certain emotions once again. In some cases I was able to open up, loving harder than I had loved before. I jumped into my new friendships with both feet blindly, despite warnings from others.

I had trust issues going in, but I trusted God to protect me. I had trust that he wouldn't allow anyone to hurt me so soon after dealing with the divorce and the betrayal from my past friendships. I had faith in my own intuition regardless of the caution from others. I was sadly mistaken but walked away with rich lessons.

It took about a year for the smoke to clear and my vision was crisp. After realizing that life has its down moments. I had people to be there for the celebrations, but they were nowhere to be seen when life got real. I do not do pity parties so I wouldn't expect them to sit around and hold my hand singing "Kum Ba Yah" by any means, but real friends are there for the good and the bad. During my down times, I was left without a call to ask, "Are you OK?" from the ones I expected it from most. They didn't owe me anything nor was I keeping track of their gestures, but it gets obvious when life's down moments bring you to your knees and you realize that it's just you and God and the people you thought were your friends are out celebrating and didn't pause to say someone is missing from the equation. Those moments showed me my value to them. In those moments the messages I had hoped for from them came from those I least expected it from, and because of the small gesture these others still hold value to me now.

Once the blinders came off during my down time away from them and I could see clearly, I began to notice other things in their behaviour that made me uneasy: the manner in which they dealt with others, talking down to others like they were better, or how they discussed people when they were not around that they claimed to be their friends. I made the call to step back and acknowledge that they had served their season.

A new season had come and I needed to surround myself with those that valued me as much as I appreciated them. I needed to have those in my circle that treated everyone well, not just when it benefited them. I needed realistic friends that were there for the ups and the downs. There needs to be balance. I was growing as a person and felt it was time to move on. Love in any relationship needs to be give and take. It isn't 50/50 but 100/100. I needed to be around those that could consistently keep it 100!

Even though those seasonal people are not friends with me today, I give thanks for the moments that we shared, the lessons they were placed there to teach me. The experience helped me discover my own self-worth. I realized that they may not have seen my value, but I was certainly able to find more of it.

In the process of separating from them, I became more independent. I acknowledged how much I had actually been able to accomplish without their help and support. This gave me the push I needed to move forward on my own. I was appreciative of the moments we had shared, but the motivation to be stronger and love Makini more was the best part.

This brings us to the "lifetime" people, which I call my foundation. I had spent time healing and keeping my inner circle small after the divorce with my sisters and three male friends who had been there for me since high school. I have been fortunate enough to have my core circle of lifetime-ers. It is said that you attract what you are, and if I am anything like many of the people in my life that are recent or that have been around for decades, I'm happy with who I am. They are like candles that light up the world. A thousand candles can be lit by one single candle. It doesn't weaken the light through sharing; it remains just as bright while serving a purpose. They make me strive to be a candle, unlike the matchstick that burns out quickly and eventually has no use. Most things in life are built from the ground up. You need solid foundation to support or else the smallest shake can cause it to crumble.

My most valued supporters for some reason all happen to be of the opposite-sex: stand-up men who have never taken advantage of me even when the opportunity was there. During my separation, I had one or two incidents when I consumed too much alcohol in my emotional state and was treated like their baby sister and taken care of with the utmost respect. I know men who, if placed in the same situation, would not have done the same.

On numerous occasions they have gone above and beyond the call of duty for my children and me. These friendships carried me most during my divorce and gave me hope that not all men are vial creatures. At a time when I was afraid to trust and afraid to date because I had been hurt, betrayed, and broken, they helped me heal.

These bonds began to form in my first year of high school or shortly before. Over time they have developed as we matured and blossomed into friendships that I couldn't imagine myself without. Effort has been made on both sides to maintain what we have built and that's important. I genuinely care for them and their well-being, and I know that they feel the same. People can say they care, but you know it's real by how they make you feel.

With them, I'm never alone. They are there for me when I want to laugh or cry about a situation. They show their presence for both birthdays and funerals. They have kept it consistent with letting me see that they can be counted on for both the ups and the down times.

Having a support system is important when life gets rough. We all face adversities and need motivation to keep pushing or else our insecurities and fears can take advantage. A support system provides practical or moral support when needed. Our network of supportive relationships helps us to acquire and maintain success in life.

As with all relationships, the lifetime relationships take time and effort. They can be challenging to establish, have their disappointing moments, but are well worth every bit of it. It has been most appreciated when I don't have to ask for support, but I know that I have people I can ask should I be brave enough to put my ego aside. Asking for help isn't easy for many, but understand that God placed people into our lives for a reason. It isn't a sign of weakness, so we can be open to receiving help.

These relationships leave us feeling stronger. They help us to grow. They can re-establish competence. At times when I felt high stress starting out in real estate or during my divorce, when I felt moments of high anxiety and the demands of my life seemed too much, the support of my lifetime friends helped me cope and return to the level at which I should be functioning. Spending quality time in the presence of positive people doing activities to distract me or having productive conversations about my situation to put my mind in solution-mode made a world of difference in keeping my eyes on my goals.

They have contributed to the development of new skills with their support and friendship. Positively challenging me at times when I found myself in new situations. Not only were they teachers but also models of how to cope in times when I wasn't functioning at full capacity.

Their contributions have allowed me to achieve some of my greatest goals. We can be in business for ourselves, but we can't do it alone. Leveraging their skills and resources that I do not have, or, at times, do not have the desire to have, has allowed me to achieve objectives I could not have on my own. Together we have grown in our personal lives and in business.

After experiencing much hurt and betrayal, it took me some time to realize that I also needed the connections of value from women. I needed female peers, business partners, network associates, friends, and even my sisters. Once I saw the value I was missing from secluding myself from these connections, I sought out female social settings and groups that helped me regain trust in women.

We get so wrapped up in our own personal problems and busy lives that we don't take the time to nurture ourselves and grow meaningful relationships. Thanks to technology we get caught up in connecting via text or social media, quickly forgetting how valuable face-to-face contact can be. We bypass the human relation of a facial expression or tone of voice that can warm the heart.

Women need to nurture, empower, and edify each other. They can do so in many ways including:

RELIEVE STRESS – Bonding with other women is a biological response to soothing ourselves when faced with stress. When women are stressed, the hormone oxytocin is released, causing an immediate desire to seek and maintain relationships.

When I'm faced with a tough day, an evening with my girls is like a dose of medicine.

BE ACCOUNTABILITY PARTNERS – Choose someone that has similar goals and dreams. Be sure it's someone who cares about your success—someone you can trust to give objective opinions.

I have an accountability partner for all areas of my life, from work, church, and the gym.

PROVIDE CONSTRUCTIVE CRITICISM – You need people who love you enough to be able to tell you the truth when you need to hear it. When you have your blinders on, they can tell you objectively that you're making a not-so-smart decision and they have nothing to gain when calling you out on your crap.

I have a dear friend who holds no other mutual friends. Her constructive criticism has always been welcomed and she gives it to me daily. She calls me out when I'm acting out of character, and we search for the reason why.

BE A NURTURING SUPPORT SYSTEM – Women are natural nurturers. Having nurturing relationships that are give and take outside of your blood relations is a must. Friends don't have to love you; they choose to. When you give and receive female empowerment and support, it feels good to see each other shine.

A girlfriend of mine used to run a group home and loves to be the mother hen. She is one of the most supportive people I know, and she empowers and supports all that I do, and I love her for it.

ALSO NOTE THAT:
One person can't fulfill all your needs – No one person is perfect, so it's unfair to put all your eggs in one basket. Having different people, you connect with helps meet your emotional, social, and physical needs.

I have different friendships to fulfil different needs. My male friends can't fulfill the same needs as my female friends.

Friends help you live longer – Research studies have found that when you have healthy social networks you live a longer, happier, and healthier life. These connections help you live a fuller sense of purpose and have a more positive view on life.

My life wouldn't be the same without the people in it. Thanks to the support system of my friends and family, I have been resilient in the face of adversity. From the time I became a teenage mother until today when I'm having ups and downs in real estate, I've been blessed to always have someone there cheering me on and in some cases saving me from drowning. For every hurtful situation I have been fortunate to have found joy in knowing that there is always one person out there that loves me enough to want to see me succeed. Cherish the friendships that grow with you the most. Be LOVE. Show LOVE. Receive LOVE.

- LOSS -

If there is one thing in this life that is inevitable, it's death. At some point, sooner or later, we all will lose a loved one and experience a grief so intense that a dagger to the heart may not be a description suitable enough to paint a picture of the feeling. The more significant the loss, the more intense grief you will experience. Grief is a totally natural response to loss. It's the emotional suffering you feel when someone you love dies.

After the loss of a loved one, it can be hard for many to pick up the pieces, heal the wounds, and carry on living. How we deal with it varies not only by person but also by the situation. I know this all too well. I lost two very significant people in my life within roughly a year of each other but dealt with each one completely differently. How we grieve depends on your life experience, personality, coping style, the deceased's level of significance in your life, and your faith.

I lost my sister, Andrea, who was probably the only constant throughout my life, and my grandmother, who helped raise me from the time I was in kindergarten. Both losses were sudden and happened in such a similar manner it was almost unreal to experience twice in such a short period of time.

My sister was practically my twin but with a seven-year age difference. Andrea was my only sister of many that shared both mother and father. Aries babies that sounded the same, thought the same, laughed the same, and even had the same facial features. Only difference, she was more outspoken than I was. Our mother always referred to her as my lawyer. Andrea never missed the opportunity to speak up for me when I was too shy or timid to speak my mind.

Growing up she would even speak up for me against our own mother when I was too afraid. My sister taught me how to stand up for myself and how to speak what I wanted or else no one would know what I was thinking. When I was in elementary school and had bullies pick on me, she always came to the rescue, not just in my defense but she also made sure I understood how to defend myself should I come across the scenario again.

We purchased our first home together. My sister was there for the birth of all my children. Andrea was a staple in my life for every event I can think of that mattered. Her name was my first word for goodness sake! My mother recalls my chanting of her name "A-gea." The bond we had was that of Siamese twins. I felt my husband got jealous of her when I was married as we were always on the phone when we couldn't be together.

During my divorce, my sister was there for me 110 percent. She even served my husband the divorce papers. Andrea was the one I would speak to when I needed to vent. She helped me with my kids during that rough time in my life. She even moved in for six month during my separation to help me cope. Having her there was like replacing a leg on a broken chair. I didn't feel stable without her.

The summer after my divorce was a hot, humid one. My kids struggled with their asthma and many others I knew had difficulty as well due to the weather. One morning my niece hinted to me that her mother was having trouble breathing and refused to get it checked out. I phoned my sister immediately to make sure she was OK. The stubborn Aries that she is assured me she would consult a doctor after we attended church that day if it didn't improve.

During church service, we sat together as usual, yet she was unusually quiet. Her fearless spirit seems scared. We held hands, prayed, hugged, and shed a few tears. Nothing was majorly out of the ordinary that day, but she did walk noticeably slower as she returned from making her offering at the altar. Expressing her chest pain and difficulty breathing, she still seemed calm. By the end of service, she notified me that she had difficulty breathing and we decided to stay back a while until she was able to walk to the car.

By the time we reached our cars, Andrea said she was ready to see a doctor. In my heart I wanted to be the one to take her to the emergency room, but I had been arguing with my ex-husband about him not wanting to return my son and was instructed by the police to wait at home until further notice. My sister decided to reach out to my mother for the support, and I asked them both to keep me posted on any changes.

Later that evening I was told they would be keeping her for observation. It had been a long day of drama and excitement. I sent my sister a text: "Coming in the morning. Hard f#$%*@& Day." As always her supportive spirit replied: "That's OK sunshine. Rest see you tomorrow." Little did I know that would be my last text from her.

That night I slept curled up next to my son and was awakened by my phone. My baby sister was calling asking if I could drive to the hospital. They had called requesting a family member to come. Never in my wildest dreams did I assume it was something serious. I lived about a 45-minute drive during morning rush hour away from where she was and thought if I went straight after dropping my son to daycare then I could skip traffic. When I received the second call asking me to hurry up even before I could make it to the daycare, I knew it was serious.

My baby sister made it to the hospital before me and called back to let me know that Andrea had gone into cardiac arrest and was in an induced coma. By the time I made it to the hospital, my family was in the waiting room of the Intensive Care Unit waiting for the doctor to give us an update. The update was not much when it came. She was induced into a coma to protect the brain. We were told they would stop the meds after 24 hours, and she would wake up. As a family, we sat there in the waiting room to support each other.

The next morning, we all returned to await our sleeping beauty. My mother, father, grandmother, sisters, brothers, cousins, aunts, etc. were all present. We dominated the waiting room as we took turns throughout the day sitting at her bedside. When there was still no sign of her waking up the next day, we began to worry. Andrea's blood pressure skyrocketing and the life support machines going off were too much for my heart to bear. Her eyes seemed as though they wanted to open, and the nurses warned us that her flickering eyelids was a sign she was soon to wake.

I sat by her praying she would wake and rubbing her arms. The nurse on her other side talked in her ear as she adjusted her pillow and looked at me with sad eyes. My sister's eyes popped open for a second and as much as they said she wasn't conscious, she saw me. She stared into my eyes for the last time. The entire 30 seconds I froze as we spoke in silence with our eyes. Then they shut and all I could do was cry. She said so much at that moment with her eyes, but I did not know then that she had said good-bye.

Word got out that Andrea was in a coma, and visits from childhood friends piled in. They were coming from a funeral of another friend. All dressed in black. The hospital hallway and waiting room began to fill with bodies dressed in mourning. I could not stay another minute. It seemed as if they had come to say their farewells.

My heart broke.

I was told her blood pressure climbed that night and she was sent for more tests. The next morning a family meeting was called and the doctor told us there was bleeding in the brain and signs of brain damage. If she was to wake, she would never be the same.

I had always felt that my family had a strong faith in God, but at that moment it was being tested. We refused to believe that as much as she loved God and served him that he would let her go this way. We refused to believe that the doctor had the final say; he was not God. We believed if we prayed hard, if we had the prayers of everyone else, he would let her wake and return unharmed. Stranger things have happened to people in comas.

Day in and day out, we gathered as a family at the hospital taking shifts at her bedside. We researched what we knew. We studied her medical records. We questioned doctors. We contacted medical professionals in other countries that had practically worked miracles before. We prayed relentlessly. As a family we refused to give up on our angel here on earth. For three weeks we held onto her and declined to submit to what the doctors had diagnosed.

Andrea's organs began to shut down. Her skin color had darkened. Her tongue had swollen until her mouth couldn't shut. We had lost the fight. The doctors declared her legally dead.

I had never thought it possible to physically feel my heart break. Sitting in the hospital boardroom with many of my siblings, my parents, my grandmother, nieces, sister-in-law, and even church family as the doctor broke the news, it hit hard and it hit us all at once. It was almost impossible to know who to console first as we all broke out crying in unison.

That had to be the hardest emotional moment in my life. Do I console my niece, an only child who just lost her mother whose father doesn't live in the country? Do I console my father who just lost his firstborn? Do I console my mother who just lost her eldest daughter? My thoughts at that moment revolved around my hurting family and healing their hearts. As much as my heart was hurting, I felt then that my sister and I said our good-byes in that final stare down the Wednesday morning.

Andrea's passing broke me for some time. It broke my family. Together we cried at the altar at church. For weeks, my eyes were swollen from crying myself to sleep. Post-traumatic stress hit us like a bag of bricks. A handful of us had a hard time trying to recover from the three weeks of sleeping beauty's coma. We had experienced many deaths before, but none affected us like this.

It was only my second year as a licensed realtor and I was doing it full-time. I was on a roll before my sister Andrea went into cardiac arrest. My business came to a halt. I had reliable real estate agents that were taking my calls and emails, but I didn't care. For four months I wasn't able to handle business. I mentally wasn't able to function normally. I was hurting and barely had the strength to take care of my children much less run a business.

During my divorce, my sister was my rock, and I had the ability to keep my momentum going and maintain focus to succeed. When she died, I hit rock bottom. The only thing I had strength for was church on Sundays. I felt her there, and it gave me peace. For the remainder of the summer, my days consisted of daily visits to my mother's house to make sure she was good. My brother and I would be there daily to console her and each other. We tried to keep her company as our businesses went down the drain. Most of our visits were filled with storytelling of the joy she brought us, the jokes she gave, and the good times shared.

It took time to heal and it took effort. It started in my mind and carried into my actions. My sister was such a happy, loving person. We even chose to wear white at her send-off. She wouldn't want to see us suffering and mourning while the businesses she watched us build went down the drain. She wouldn't allow us to be stuck for so long if it were someone else who had passed.

Andrea's positive words began to play in my head, and I would post them as statuses on Facebook as she once did. Her infectious giggle would echo in my ears and make me smile. I would pray and hear her voice in my head praying right along with me. My prayers began to strengthen, my attitude began to change, and my heart began to swell when people would call or text saying my positive posts reminded them of her.

Losing my sister completely changed my life whether I wanted it to or not. For over 30 years I had someone there to hold my hand and rub my back. I had her back through thick and thin, and she had mine. Without her, I was forced to be strong on my own. I was forced to recognize the strength that God had given me from day one but I didn't exercise.

Although I was independent, that voice that said, "Who cares what they think? Keep it moving. We got this!" when I felt I had failed was not on the other end of the phone to lift my spirits or restore my faith. The voice of reassurance hadn't left me completely. God speaks when we take the time to listen. I took months to just be still. "Listen to advice and accept instruction, that you may gain wisdom in the future" (Proverbs 19:20).

Everyone may require a different amount of time to heal. No one can force your actions; you have to be ready. There is no normal length of time to grieve. Some people could take weeks, others months, or even years. It's a natural process that unfolds at its own pace.

My sister was not only a positive force in my life, but after her passing I learned she was for many others also. After her passing, I was overwhelmed by the phone calls and messages from others that felt I needed to hear how special she was and how she affected their lives. I realized then that I too wanted to be remembered for affecting lives when I leave this earth. She and I may have worn the same shoe size, but I wasn't about to try to fill her shoes. I had my own stilettos to grow into.

I wanted to crawl into a hole and die when I first lost Andrea. My sister was the hub of the family and her strength displayed at times was greater than most men I know. I did not feel I displayed that strength until I lost her. I discovered that many people were now looking to me to take on her powers, to try and solve their issues, and I didn't think I could fill those shoes.

Her inspiring posts on social media became one small area that I embraced to help me heal. Making the daily effort to uplift another seemed to alleviate some of the stress. Her ability to help another in need without hesitation became a trait that I enjoyed mimicking. My sister made the effort to show her face at important functions of loved ones when she could and gave a hand when needed. I too began to make those efforts and found much joy in building my connections after losing one with her.

The more pressure that was put on me to be more like Andrea, the more I looked to God for help. I learned to pray harder, to pray more frequently, to pray with gratitude without asking for anything. I acknowledged him even when I felt he wasn't listening. Each day I felt just a little bit stronger. Each day I tackled through things I never believed possible without her. My loved ones would praise my strength and encouragement, which became motivation to continue healing through perseverance. Healed people heal people.

Losing my grandmother about a year after my sister was extremely hard. The family was still recovering from funeral costs, some were still grieving, and I barely had time to catch my breath. She passed in the similar way that we lost my sister. She had a stroke and was home alone for a short time. My mother came in from buying groceries to find her on the floor. When I got the call to go to the hospital, I was shocked to hear she was in a coma.

I thought God had a serious sense of humour. I thought about my mother's mental health if she lost her mother a year after losing her daughter and what that would do to the rest of the family. I envisioned how she would feel and knew it had to be much worse than what I could possibly feel.

When I arrived to the emergency room to get the update, I had more hope than what I had the previous year arriving to the ICU for my sister. My grandmother was functioning. She was sleeping but half of her body was reacting. She would scratch her nose, rub her head, and even push the nurse away when she tried to adjust her intravenous tubes. The doctor informed us that the stroke had caused damage to one half of her body, but the other was doing well.

My hope became weak after a few days. My grandmother's movements became less and less frequent. The doctors' tests showed bleeding in the brain as my sister had experienced. I didn't need to be psychic to understand what came next if it didn't stop. My prayer switched from healing and wonders for my grandmother to strength and healing for my mother.

Feelings of deep sympathy and sorrow came over me. My mother was still grieving over the loss of her daughter; how was she going to handle losing her mother who had been her best friend for the past two and a half decades? She had brought my grandparents to Canada in 1988 after Hurricane Gilbert destroyed the family home that she was raised in. Since then she took care of her mother, especially after the death of her father in 1991. They were partners that lived together and did everything together.

I was consumed by compassion for my mother that I distracted my own feelings of grief for a while. I wanted to help. I wanted to do everything I possibly could to help my mother, but I wasn't even sure how to do that. My mother had always displayed such emotional strength that even if she was hurting, we couldn't see it. She had a good game face. But this time I could see through it. Strong women like her often encourage others and get overlooked for encouraging when they need it. I wanted her to know I was there for her.

I got the call to come to the hospital because my grandmother had eventually gone brain dead and passed away. The hurt in my heart wasn't as deep as it was the year before. I tried at first to understand it and came up with the fact that my grandmother, although youthful, was in her nineties. She had lived a very long and full life. She played a major role in my life. I didn't love her any less than my sister, and we possibly lived together longer than I had with my Andrea.

Possibly I had come to terms with it because I expected death at 90 versus 39. Maybe I was still numb from the grief of losing my sister the year before. Whatever the reason, I was at peace with God for his decision to call my grandmother home. It's possible I had learned from the past experience and was able to handle it much better and maintain momentum while grieving. I like to say it's my last memory of her that keeps me smiling.

The first 48 hours seemed like déjà vu, but I refused to have a repeat of that experience again. I loved her dearly, but she lived a full life of over 90 years, and I had the happy memory of us dancing in church just 24 hours before her stroke.

This was a woman that helped raise me since I was in kindergarten. She was patient, kind, gentle, and strong. She made the choice not to keep many friends and distractions in her life and seemed very at peace with that. All of her relationships were those of quality. She too left me with changes to make in my life to better myself and those around me when I thought about what made her happy in life. My grandmother was rich in love, joy, and peace. She showed me that love is the selfless giving of oneself. That joy is the inner celebration of producing structural strength. And she showed me that peace is a still quietness in the face of life.

I focused on the quality not the quantity of those around me. The friends I kept close were reduced significantly in numbers, and I wanted only those that gave me peace to consume my time. I made a valid effort to reduce the amount of distractions of drama/negativity in my life as well. Parties without purpose lost their excitement. If it was not to celebrate a birthday or special occasion, it felt like wasted time that I could never regain.

I was able to cope much quicker this time. Dealing with my grief this time around may not have been as hard, but the compassion for my mother took most of my energy. When my sister died, I felt we were all hurting at the same level of pain. With my grandmother, I strongly felt my mother bared the most pain. Their bond was the closest of the nine children my grandmother had bared, and I felt my mother had made the most amounts of life sacrifices for her.

My mindset for this loss was very different. I had grown as a person, developed more faith, and accepted God's will. I believe those factors helped. Had I not have gone through the challenges of dealing with the grief of losing my sister, things may have turned out differently. This leads me to believe I definitely gained strength from my experience.

LOSS

Chapter 8

- CHANGE WILL TRANSFORM YOUR LIFE -

Change means to transform or convert. In order to make positive changes in your life you must transform your current way of thinking, your current way of acting. You must convert to a new model. Shift your paradigm from the old to the new and elevate your life. We cannot change our problems using the same mindset and habits that created them. Our old familiar ways prevent us from the future we were designed to have.

It has often been said that there are two important days in our lives: the day we are born and the day we find out why. After the death of my marriage, my friendships, my sister, and then my grandmother, I was in desperate need of change to find purpose. I needed to add more meaning to my life. I did not just want change in my surroundings but also change in my mindset. I wanted to change what my priorities and focus in life were. I was done with the patterns of my past.

If I wasn't physically contributing to the negatives, I had to have been in my thoughts and the energy I was letting off. I was done with being forced to change through negative experiences. I wanted to make choices of change on my own voluntarily. I wanted to make transformations that were the will of God. I needed to meet God halfway by doing the work.

Mindset is a powerful thing. Our mind controls so much of what we do and what we receive out of life. The traffic of the mind can lead to the wreck of life or the destiny of life. It will build you or it will break you, depending on where your head is. I was all over the place in my mind at one point and realized I had to set goals and remain focused on them or else the changes I was making wouldn't be sustainable enough for my growth to the end of my journey. Everyone gets discouraged and wants to give up, even great leaders and the most successful, but having a goal gives the emotional attachment for you to make the needed changes and reach those goals.

Change in my level of faith

To begin, I changed the way I prayed. I made my prayers more specific and had more intent when I released them. Prayers are like affirmations; if we hear it often enough we believe in them. They are our words to God, but they help keep us grounded and keep us focused on our goals when they are said with intent. Whether things are good or bad, I pray. I say a prayer not wishes, because I believe in God not genies.

Whether the intent is to ask for or thank for, I pray. "O Jerusalem, I have set intercessors, on your walls who shall cry to God all day and all night for your fulfillment of his promises. Take no rest, all you who pray, and give God no rest until he establishes Jerusalem and makes respected and admired throughout the earth" (Isaiah 62:6).

I found peace in going to church with my family and learning more about God. I found strength in the messages preached to my weekly. It affected how I felt about my week and gave me the courage to get through the week's challenges. I didn't feel the same if I missed a Sunday. My pastor Orim Meikle had a way of speaking to my spirit. I connected with his delivery of the word, and his passionate style of preaching lit something on the inside of me every time. I began taking notes in service and made the conscious effort to live a better life. It inspires me: helping others, giving back, loving more, and living out the church's motto, "changing and affecting lives."

At the end of every service, as a congregation, we say:

"We believe and we agree that God has called us, and he has empowered us to change and affect every life. I believe and I agree that God has called me, and he has empowered me to change and affect every life."

I didn't just repeat those words but I let them seep into my subconscious so I could be a doer of the words.

My eldest sister was the reason I began attending that church on a regular basis. Although my mother made sure church was a part of our lives growing up, it was my sister that insisted I attended my current church as she felt it would connect with me on a deeper level. Her passing opened my eyes to things in and out of the church. It also opened my ears. When my pastor or his wife is preaching, I not only listen attentively but I hear the words clearly. At a time when some would have lost faith in God, I chose to seek him further. Believing in his power and strength changed my life. When I was weak, God gave me strength.

When times are bad, my faith keeps me going. It allows me the power of knowing that things will not stay in that state forever. This too shall pass. It is the motivation that empowers me to not give up. I was in church and a woman said, "When times are rough and it seems dark, don't feel that it's because God has left you. He is saving you from harm and protecting you under the shadow of his wings." Appreciate all of life and the experiences it brings.

Being grateful for others and showing more love has strengthened the relationships that already existed and helped build new ones. I value my relationships very much. My pastor and his wife inspire me. I look up to them both as mentors and have a great deal of love and respect for them. My sister's passing left me with the desire to want to give my best to others. God has blessed us with gifts to bless others. In turn, I have become happier with my life and those that remain in it.

Change in relationships

Where we live, our environment, and the people close to us have a lot to do with who we become. Part of my changes included limiting who I was around and where I went. Setting boundaries became liberating. I walked away from people and things that served little purpose in my life. If someone is not adding to you, they are taking away. I had to remove them from the equation.

I started one night with a clean up of my Facebook account. Social media can be a blessing and a curse at the same time. It keeps us plugged in and connected. I went through the list of people on my friends list and unfriended the negative, dramatic, energy vampires. I wanted no association. Not only did I not care to see the lack of constructiveness, but I didn't care for their friendship. It's OK to unfriend people in real life. If neither party is adding value to the other, there isn't a need.

I no longer felt obligated to remain acquaintances or friends. I felt OK with the decision to let go and not look back. I lost the guilt of feeling I had missed someone's party. I lost the pressure of feeling like I needed to be everywhere. What I gained was more important. I gained quality in the relationships I hold dear to my heart. I gained peace of mind. The clutter of thoughts and worries became less and less.

I was once a person that gave too much energy to what others would think or what they would say about my life. I realized that no matter how good of a person you are or no matter how much you do for others, there will forever be those that don't like you and will have something to say. They will have some judgement to make, some remark to pass. Not everyone is going to like you, but not everyone matters. The minute I began saying "Who cares?" was the moment I began living freely. It's not that I don't care, but really what is there to care about. Their issue is not with me; it's with themselves.

After my divorce, I changed the type of men I would accept invitation for dates from and, if I allowed them to stay, I changed how much of my life I would change when they walked into it. My last two relationships were roughly eight and half years each, taking up 17 years of my life, and I lost who I was during those times by revolving my life around them. I loved wholeheartedly but gave up my true being in the process. Loving hard isn't a bad thing as long as you love yourself hard in the process.

Self-love wasn't a thought during those years. My focus was on loving those around me and making sure I was fulfilling what I thought to be my womanly duties in the relationship. I made sure the happiness of others was above my own, forgetting that if I wasn't happy, how could I truly make another person happy. I didn't have balance. Today, I focus on myself and my children, and whomever God chooses to bring to me will add to that, not take away.

I'm no longer looking for a partner because, as much as I hate to admit it, I'm attracted to the things that don't last. If God sends me someone, I'll know. I'm learning to value those that God brings into my life and accept them for who and where they are in life. I feel I lack patience and believe being part of the microwave generation has me wanting it all instantly. I've come to understand that things work on God's time not our time. I am learning to listen for the direction instead of pushing things into the direction I want. I'm learning to be more patient on building relationships so they will last. "Wherefore judge nothing before the time, until the Lord come, who will both bring to light the hidden things of darkness, and make manifest the counsels of the hearts" (1 Corinthians 4:5).

A good relationship supports you, loves you, and makes you happy. A bad one relies on you, expects from you, and makes you unhappy. We need to believe that we are worthy of love if we ever expect to fully experience love and belonging. Don't ever allow your goals to be derailed because of someone else. You should be helping and encouraging each other's goals and aspirations. Your personal and even your business success are dependent on the person you choose to be in a relationship with. If you want to grow together, reach for those goals together.

We are wired as humans to love and to be loved in every possible way. When our needs are not met, we don't function as we should. We break and fall apart. We become numb, we ache, and become sick. Then we hurt others.

How you feel about the person you're in a relationship with should reflect in your actions. When we don't show love in our actions to the people we claim to love, it takes a lot out of us and takes away from them. You can say "I Love You" as many times a day as you want; if your actions don't show it, those words hold no weight. It's important to practice the love you profess. The behaviour when your partner is in your presence is important, but so is the behaviour when your partner is not around.

Your life is more valuable than people just showing up for the position. People are not just placed into your life for no reason. No matter the type of relationship, you should be heard in all things. There should be an understanding at all times. You should be valued for who you are. And you should be respected for what you bring to the table. Relationships matter...my relationship with God, my family, and those God brings into my life.

Change in mindset

I first had to unlearn everything I had learned before. I had to clear my mind and become a sponge for new knowledge and growth. I raised my belief in myself, and it raised the results I received in return from life.

There was a time in my life when the only reading I did was magazines and social media statuses. I had changed my environment to obtain a difference and surrounded myself with people I could learn from, but where I got lost in being a student was reading books—not just any book, but books that would help in my growth process. Self-help books and spiritual books caught most of my attention.

Reading self-help books does not mean that something is wrong with you; it means that you want to grow and become a better person. Learning from great motivational speakers who are living or who have passed on and left legendary literature are just as great as mentors speaking at seminars. One of the greatest motivational speakers of all time is God. Reading his word and studying the life nuggets that have been left for us is something I do daily.

My day begins by reading a scripture and my daily devotion after prayers when my eyes open each morning. This has set the tone for how my day is going to start and trickles down into my day. It affects my mindset and my mood. It sets the tone and motivates me to be a better person.

My day ends with reading a chapter or two from other great motivators who decided to put their thoughts on paper. Authors like Bob Proctor, Napoleon Hill, and Joyce Meyer have changed lives around the world. I have also allowed them to change mine. How do you change your mindset, you ask? You first make the decision. The rest will follow.

I made the choice to change my mindset, and like a magnet things that I needed to make things happen began to appear. What we focus on we attract. I focused on making the effort to change and the changes started happening. Yes, it's that simple.

During my divorce, a friend of mine sat down with me to watch the legendary film The Secret that featured Bob Proctor, who is known for mastering the law of attraction. He teaches people how to understand their hidden abilities to do more, be more, and have more in every area of life. I followed his teaching on social media to gain inspiration from quotes that were posted regularly.

I made vision boards, goal cards, and tried to focus on being positive to attract more positivity into my life. My belief was up and down, but once I raised my belief in his teachings and mindset something happened. It started with more and more people around me mentioning his name and doing vision boards, vision journals, and being mindful of what they put into the universe.

One day a friend of mine began to brag that she was going to be published by the same publisher that had once published Bob and suggested I do the same. A few weeks later another friend called in complete excitement that they had just got off a call with Bob himself. Another friend had connected the call, but his excitement was that of a man that had won the lottery. Shortly after that, I signed a book deal with the publisher that had once worked with Bob.

Approximately five months after that, I received a phone call as I sat at my desk at work. The man on the other end of the phone tried to quickly explain that we didn't know one another, but he had connected with me on the social networks and wanted to invite me to hear Bob Proctor speak the following day at no cost. I immediately thought this was a prank and tried to get off the phone. "Can you email me the details? I'm in the middle of something and my cell battery is dying," I said in attempt to end the call.

Within seconds, I received an email notification. It was from the man I had just brushed off. In the email were a picture of him and Bob Proctor and the details of the location where Bob was going to be speaking to an intimate group of people. I closed the email and went back to work.

My old mindset would have continued and not opened that email again, as it seemed too good to be true and too weird at the same time. As I continued working, my mind was curious. I was interested in hearing Bob speak live, I was intrigued since it wasn't going to cost me, but I was skeptical by the call from a complete stranger.

My woman's senses were all over the map. I wondered if it was a trick. I wondered if it was safe to go alone. My paradigms were trying to push back the opportunity. I wanted to go but came up with every excuse why I should not. I decided to RSVP and accept, and if I changed my mind then I could do so, but I really didn't feel compelled to decline.

Just 30 minutes before it was time to leave to hear Bob speak the next day I made the decision. I was going to attend but set up a security plan. I let two people close to me know where I was going and I would have my cell phone glued to my hand.

I arrived just in time. As I walked into the conference room, Bob Proctor himself was standing at the door. Our eyes met and made four, and I froze. Then I heard my name being called by a strange voice. I snapped out of it, and the stranger that had invited me shook my hand and said "Nice to meet you. Let me introduce you to Bob."

As I shook the hand of one of the greatest motivational speakers alive today, I thought how grateful I was that I was working on changing my mindset and accepted the invitation to meet him. I had a million reasons why I could have said no. I had a million and one reasons why I could have cancelled. Too many times we miss the opportunity and the door God opens for us based on our own fear and stupidity and blame him for not doing what he promised.

I was told to take a seat in a room of four round tables. There must have been about 30 others in the room. As I looked around at the people that had already been seated, all engulfed in what looked like deep conversation; I just wanted to observe. My introverted personality chose the only empty table hoping to blend in and leave once the evening was over.

Within minutes I had company. I was joined by two other ladies. I smiled and introduced myself hoping not to be disturbed any further after that. The two women began to converse and I played with my phone as I listened. My ears opened as I realized whom I was sitting with. I was sitting with Bob Proctor's wife! Linda Proctor.

She asked us about our lives and what we do for a living. She seemed genuinely interested in our stories. If I had not accepted my story and owned it at the time, I would have been embarrassed to share. "I'm a single mother of three children. I'm divorced from a verbally/emotionally abusive man. Currently providing for my children by selling real estate." I blurted out the Coles Notes version of my life all in one breath.

Linda Proctor's response was not what I had expected from a woman of her calibre. Not that I even knew what to expect because I had never had a conversation with a multimillionaire about my personal life. She found it inspiring. We furthered the conversation and Linda expressed how brave I had to be to decide to not only leave the marriage but to be supporting my children on a commission-based income.

"Hey Bob! Come and hear these two ladies' inspiring story." Linda says as she latches on to her husband's arm. I didn't quite have the time to process what was happening before Bob Proctor himself sat across from me at the table and asked me to retell my story. I retold it with confidence knowing that I could not have done so six months to a year prior. I would have been embarrassed and ashamed.

I had changed my mindset and that had given me confidence. If they wanted to pass judgement on me based on me telling my story then that was on them. I was proud of how far I had come. I was being transparent, laying out my past to total strangers. I pretty much said this is who I am and this is what I've been through so they can see how far I've come. Our past is important only so people can see where God has pulled us from.

Bob and Linda had to be the greatest at confidence boosting. They made me feel special, superhero special. If I weren't a humble person that encounter could have gone to my head. As Linda got up to speak and introduce her husband to the room, I thought to myself, "What would the old Makini have done?" But before I could answer that Linda announces to the entire room, "You should hear the incredible inspiring stories of the two ladies I'm sitting with."

At the end of the evening I had left there feeling like a new person. Not only was Bob's speech impeccable, but after he spoke I was able to have more personal conversation with the powerful couple before I returned home. I wasn't sure if I would ever see either of them again; either way they had helped me feel confident in my story.

I felt brand new when I reviewed the events of the evening. In addition to the experience, my takeaways from Bob's speech were in alignment with the changes I was already making and he confirmed I was on the right track to having a successful life. I just needed to tweak a few things in my habits. It's one thing to be open to listening and learning, but how are you going to apply it.

My new habits of success consist of reading/studying daily. Studying each day how to become a better me has not only made a significant difference in how I think, how I act, how I speak, but also it has allowed me the ability to understand why other people act in the manner of which they do. It removes judgment on my part when I can break down perception and character. We should always be learning to keep the mind sharp.

CHANGE WILL TRANSFORM YOUR LIFE

Having daily affirmations that we read out loud is another habit. They are positive sayings written in the present tense. If we tell ourselves a lie often enough, we start to believe it. I keep my affirmations on my office wall and in my washroom so I can see them often and read them each time I see them. The more I read them, the more I believe them. My favorite affirmation is, "I am rich in relationships and love."

Practicing to keep positive thoughts is very important. The images we create in our heads become reality. That which we focus on, we attract. When I feel a negative thought coming on, I envision a happy place, whether that is a moment with my children or lying on the beach with my girlfriends. If someone disturbs me, I wish them well. Sending love prevents negative thoughts about them and repels the negative energy from coming back in my direction. You can only attract that which is in harmony with your vibration/energy.

Setting goals is a habit of all successful people. I have long-term goals and I have short-term goals. Envision what it is that you want and be specific about it. Have dates and amounts if they're monetary-related written in the present tense in positive form. If your goal is to get out of debt, don't focus on that or it will attract more debt. Make your goal to earn a specific amount of money by a specific time and focus on that. We don't ever know how we are going to reach the goal, but pushing towards them helps us grow. Live intentionally.

Having mentors is important, even if they are people you have never met. They could be people you admire and look up to. It could be someone in your profession that is doing well or even a positive celebrity. The Proctor family has become my mentors as they are all currently contributing to my success in some way. Bob motivates daily with his posts on social media and has given me tools to keep me accountable. His wife, Linda, I see weekly, and she inspires me to push for more. Bob's daughter, Colleen, has become my coach and is helping me to share my gifts with the world instead of holding them back for myself.

And one major key to remaining successful is generosity. Share your gifts with the world. Be kind to others, be humble, spread love everywhere you go, and give back to the community. These seem like small things but have made a world of difference in my life.

The only thing constant in this world is change. Sticking to old ways and old rules has more and more book smart people failing at life. The world is constantly changing, so what makes people think that they can stay the same and succeed? Preparing myself for change rather than reacting to it has made life a lot less stressful. It has given me power and allowed me more control of the outcome. I have made mistakes and learned from them. I now make the changes to strengthen my chances of success. "And the God of all grace, who called you unto his eternal glory in Christ, after that ye have suffered a little while, shall himself perfect, establish, strengthen you" (1 Peter 5:10).

Chapter 9

- MAKING HARD DECISIONS -

Decisions, or lack of, can build you up or break you down. The mental move of making a choice can be quite difficult, especially major decisions that have strong emotional attachment and can affect your future. If you live in fear, developing the strength to make these mental moves will be very hard. Having the competence to make hard choices without being influenced by the opinions of others and listening to that gut feeling or the voice in our head (in my case God) can work out for the greater good.

I was faced with making many tough decisions, but making the choice to allow my son to try living with his father for a year was heartbreaking. I didn't fight tooth and nail in court for full custody and spend thousands of dollars to turn around and hand him over. It was a choice that only God could help me to make.

It was nearing the end of his school year for the second grade. My son's father called with a request, "Would you consider letting Kai live with me for a year?" My first thought was he was on drugs. My second thought was he was making a bad joke to get under my skin.

He wasn't serious with life right now. He was asking for my heart after he had already broken it many times before. I had to maintain my thoughts and simply tell him no.

The entire school year had been a series of visits with my son's teachers, principals, and counselors to discuss his emotional well-being. My son had adjusted well to the separation from his father and me in the beginning but was hit hard when his father had two children in the same year with his new partner. My son felt neglected and hurt. He voiced his feelings at school and it showed in his behaviour. He wasn't happy with only seeing his father four days a month, and he certainly wasn't happy about the weekends his father would call and cancel for out-of-town trips.

For every conversation we had to have to discuss our son, he would end it by asking repeatedly "Have you had a chance to think about what I asked?" or "Are you going to consider it? I promise you won't regret it." I became creative at saying no or rushing off the phone to avoid the conversation. I wasn't even going to give it a thought. How could I trust my son to a man that had easily walked out of the lives of my daughters without a second thought? How could I allow him the responsibility of parenting my son full-time when he wasn't showing responsibility of his duties on a part-time basis?

One day before the end of the school year, my son and I were having a conversation about the future. He is quite intelligent for his age, and he spoke as if I had agreed to allow him to move to his father's. I was perplexed but didn't want to say anything to make him feel closed off from the conversation. I slowly began to ask him about his wants.

Conversations of this nature weren't new to him. My son is very much a mama's boy; we discuss his emotions daily and the two of us are very affectionate. I want him to feel his feelings matter and can be discussed. So when I asked if he wanted to go and live with his father for a year I was surprised when he didn't want to answer the question. He shrugged his shoulders, looked away, and said, "I don't know."

I assured him that no matter his answer I would not be upset, that I needed to know what he wanted so his father and I could do what was best for him. I guaranteed him that whatever he said he wanted would not upset me and I would love him just the same either way. He looked me in the eyes, kissed me, and gave me a bear hug. "I love you mommy," he whispered.

I asked him again what it was that he wanted and with a painful expression he put one finger in the air and said, "Just for one year...can we try it? Please mommy."

I felt like someone had just kicked me in the chest, and I couldn't breathe. Did he just say he wanted to try living with his father? I had promised him I wouldn't get upset and as he stared at me for an answer, I knew then that I had to consider it. I had to make a sound decision not based on my feelings towards his father but based on the needs and wants of my son that was excited about bonding with his father.

They say that the most successful people in the world are quick decision-makers, but I needed to make an educated choice without emotion. I had to think about how it would affect everyone involved including my daughters. The pressure of thinking about my son's future mental health if I said no gave me anxiety. I needed God's help on this one.

I consented to a trial run over the summer to see how it affected my son mentally and emotionally. I agreed that by the end of the summer I would give a definite response to that dreaded question. I needed to make sure I was comfortable with my decision, and I was not convinced my ex-husband would show enough consistency to convince me into allowing my son to go for an entire year.

After the first month of the summer, I saw a positive change in my son. Not only was he more independent, but his confidence had grown. My son was a bright boy to begin with but his words came out with more conviction. He was excited about his new friendships with boys his age that lived in his father's area. His knowledge in the stereotypical male subjects, like cars and sports, had excelled.

The stories he would share about the bonding moments with his father made me proud. He no longer spoke of the material things he was bought in exchange for time. He spoke of moments. He shared his excitement for car games they had come up with to build his knowledge. He educated me on basketball games and players in the NBA.

That's when it hit me...I needed to do what was best for the growth of my son and allow him to go. He was blossoming by having a male role model in his life. I may not approve of everything his father does as a human being, but he is his father. I could not teach my son to be a man and the fact that I wasn't dating and there was no male role model in my household didn't help the situation. His current school wanted to pair him with a male principal or custodial agent for him to have a regular habit of learning from a man, but his father wanted to finally be that man. How could I not consider it?

There are women begging for the father of their children to participate in their lives. I was begging for this at the beginning of the separation. It would be very selfish of me not to consider the option at this point, especially after seeing the change in him after such a short time. I said nothing to anyone about what I was possibly going to do. I didn't need the opinions of others about a situation they knew little about. I didn't care for the negativity that I knew would come with comments like, "After what he did? Naw! Don't do it."

I needed God's counsel. I prayed to him about it often and asked for direction and the ability to be good with the decision once it was made. I meditated on it frequently, trusting that the right decision would come to me. "Trust in Jehovah with all thy heart, and lean not upon thine own understanding" (Proverbs 3:5).

By the time summer had ended, the insecure, overly emotional, father-deprived boy had shown much change. He was confident in himself and his abilities. Our weekend visits evolved into special bonding time and I felt closer than ever to my son, even though we had traded in our weekdays. His father convinced me that he would commit to being present and stop the overly frequent traveling and skipping out on his parental responsibility. I felt comfortable with the instruction from God that I could make the decision to let him go for a short while.

Being a mother is an amazing thing, and my children are my greatest blessings. They have humbled me and taught me how to make decisions based on how they will affect others. They expand my heart. They keep it clear to me that it's never about me; it's never about me around here. I've made many sacrifices for their happiness and don't regret any of them. Being a mother is a sacrifice lived for the service of love.

I never want my son to look back on his childhood and feel that I didn't put his needs first. I couldn't bear him asking me when he becomes an adult "Why didn't you let me have the chance to build my relationship with my father?" I love my children enough that I want them to grow up knowing that I made the best decisions for them no matter how hard it was on me emotionally.

The day before the first day of school as I'm driving to drop my son off to his father I had doubts. I questioned if I was making the right choice and whether or not I could live with making such a difficult choice. I felt in my heart that it was best for many reasons, but the emotional side of me ached. My son seemed excited, so I couldn't hurt him by changing my mind now.

After going over everything with his father, I drove away feeling empty. I was now in the car alone with my emotions. I tried to think of all the positive things that would come out of this time. This would provide extra time to bond with my daughters, the flexibility to build my business, and the freedom to date should I happen to meet someone that sparked interest. I couldn't hold in the tears. The remaining 45 minutes home, tears rolled down my face.

Had I really made such an enormous decision without any counsel of family or friends? I was intelligent enough to get advice from a lawyer, but no one I knew was aware so I was left alone with my remorse. I didn't regret it. I was just going to miss my baby.

I have nights I cry because I miss my son, but that's purely out of selfishness. I want him home, I would prefer he be with me, but I know what's best for my son and that is my priority as a mother. I was smothering him with love and affection, but I have trouble being the disciplinarian and he needs that firm treatment from his father.

Being mature enough to co-parent if given the opportunity is something I would recommend for the betterment of the children involved. I may not like my former husband as a person or the things he does, but I have seen firsthand the benefit to my child when his father and I can get along in providing his needs. We didn't work as a couple and I couldn't be happier that we ended our union, but that doesn't mean we can't still be the best parenting partners. A child who isn't fathered goes on to disrespect his or her future and dishonor it. I want the best possible future for my children and I'm willing to work with their fathers to make that happen.

Since making this decision, I feel that is has built me up as a person as well as my son. It has allowed me to put more attention on my daughters and we make plenty of it, especially since they are now teens that need guidance. It's provided me with the ability to focus on my projects for work and my women empowerment groups. I also feel it has given me a slight break in the pressure of being a single mother. An eight-year-old child requires attention, time, money, and not having the pressures of spreading myself too thin relieves some of that for the time being. I have to say that I'm confident I made the right decision.

When we are faced with tough decisions, we must get tougher. God did not create us to fail. In order to succeed we need to be able to make decision. The decision-makers of today are in control and those that cannot make decisions go absolutely nowhere.

Chapter 10

- TURN YOUR MESS INTO YOUR MESSAGE -

People remember stories. They help us feel a connection. When we hear a story it evokes emotion, memory, or a feeling. Everyone has a story. We can allow our stories to break us if we've experienced severe hard times or we can turn our mess into our message by sharing it to inspire others.

People see where you are in your life but never understand what it took for you to get there. Whether you are a successful entrepreneur, a community leader, or someone who experienced tragedy and choose to remain happy, someone is looking at you wondering how you are in that position. Your friends see good things happening for you and assume it's luck or instant recognition, not understanding that there was a process. A long list of failures and disappointments had to happen in order for you to be in your current state.

I have chosen to not only be transparent about my life experience but to also use my struggles to push me to strive for better. Pain will push you. Vision will pull you. Mine has managed to propel me. I have used my story to connect with women all over the world. I have used it to strike emotional cords to connect and to help them grow, reach their goals, and accomplish change.

No matter your age, gender, religion, race, social status, or economic level, we can all relate to someone with parts of our stories. Happiness, sadness, joy, or pain, our stories can touch a heart and build a connection with people we never thought possible. Sharing the good stories and the bad has allowed me to educate through my experience, form bonds with men and women, and give others the chance to understand why I operate in the manner in which I do.

Depending on the scenario, the people, and the topic of conversation, I always choose to tell the story that applies with the lesson I'm trying to educate on at that moment. Depending on my audience, I decide what parts of the story and how deep into detail I want to go. My focus is always to inspire. I aspire to give another hope and make them say, "Wow! If she can do that, then so can I," or even say to themselves, "My life really isn't that bad compared to what she went through."

My purpose with this book is to show that it doesn't matter where you have come from; you can accomplish great things if you put your mind to it. I started out living in government housing and now I own property with equity. I have much more real estate I'd like to acquire in the next five years, and I'm on my way to those goals. I help others to reach their goals in real estate by profession. Whether or not a person decides to purchase real estate through me, I aim to educate them with the knowledge they require to make good decisions. I share tips online and answer questions via phone call/text message every day.

I want young teenage mothers to feel that they can aspire for greatness although they made a premature choice to start a family. I hope that my story will make a difference in at least one young girl's life and if more, then I will consider that a bonus. I've done very well for myself considering where I come from and what struggles I have dealt with, which means anyone else can too. I wasn't born into money, and success wasn't handed to me. I had to do it the old-fashioned way. I worked for it, and God opened doors.

I have not had an easy life, but I have learned that an easy life is not something I would ever wish for. My trials molded me and made me unique. They have made me a better person. I have history and I allow God to control the journey. When he is in control your mistakes won't kill you. Your failures and struggles become your testimony. I view my past as my blueprint, the map to show others how far I've come and how they too can get there. The lesson is not in the mistake but how you respond. Your response to your struggles is what determines your character and where you will go in life.

Since owning my story and the trials that I have experienced, I now go out into the world and share it with others just as I have shared parts of it here with you. What they take from it is up to them and what God allows them to see. Personal development is our job; the magic that happens from it is God's job.

I am someone that enjoys laughter. I enjoy laughing and making others laugh. I enjoy being in the presence of others that make me laugh. I have had moments that others possibly look at me and think I'm crazy for laughing in that moment. I've discovered that you can't be so serious all of the time, and a little laughter can lighten the mood even when you're the only one laughing. I'm known for laughing at my own problems when things are out of my control. I think God has a sense of humour. Laughter is the medicine that soothes my soul. You have to learn to enjoy life along the way, as things are bound to happen and we can't allow them to keep us down.

The day after New Year's 2014, I was home with my eldest daughter when I discovered my basement was flooding. I was looking for the charger for my iPad and thought one of my children may have used it downstairs by the computer. As I opened the door to my walkout basement, I heard the sound of water spraying. A pipe had broken in the wall and blown off the panel that gives access to the pipe. The shut-off valve was just below the break, so shutting off the water from that location wasn't possible. The water was spraying from above and there was already about an inch of water on the carpet of my finished basement.

I looked around the room and noticed electronics plugged in all over. I had to act fast. I thought about the fire hazard and panicked for a few minutes. I screamed for my daughter to come and help me. My daughter and I unplugged everything and removed as many belongings as we could from the floor to prevent further damage.

I wasn't sure what to do or who to call. I decided to run next door to my neighbour's, the closest male I could get access to. No answer. I called the water company, the city, plumbers, and anyone else I could think of that could advise me on how to make it stop. It was a holiday and everything was closed. Most of the numbers led to voicemails about being on holidays until after New Year's Day. Any of the live voices that picked up the phone had no good advice to give. So as I watched the water continue to pour, I thought to myself, "What a way to start the new year?"

As much as I wanted to cry, I laughed. I even made a few sarcastic jokes to my daughter as we listened to the waterfalls pouring from the walls. It was out of my control. The carpet was already soaked and the damage already done. For at least an hour the water continued to pour and didn't seem like it intended to stop.

One of the company's I had contacted for help returned my call and said the water would stop when all the water from above drained out and if I turned on the laundry room taps it would help the process go faster. So I followed instructions expecting the water to stop flowing shortly after. No such luck. I checked the spraying water every few minutes to make sure the water levels stayed below the first steps.

After another 30 minutes or so, one of the plumbers returned my call. After listening to my voicemail he realized I couldn't wait until tomorrow. He informed me that my main shut-off was elsewhere and instructed me how to turn it off over the phone. The silence once the water stopped was unreal. I didn't realized how loud the sound of the water was until it stopped.

I couldn't help but laugh. All this time had passed, so much water was in my basement, and the solution was so simple yet unknown to me. I was so irritated that the first guy gave me such incorrect advice and had caused about an extra hour and a half of running water into my carpet that all I could do was laugh. The damage was done.

After that, I had spent hours trying to find a shop vac and anything else to help salvage what I could. My insurance company had someone return my call to advise me that a cleanup crew would be coming to assess and clean up the damage the following day. I was ready to cancel my plans for the night. I could have had a pity party instead. I had three friends that had come to help with the cleanup. There were enough of us for a party. I realized staying home and crying over water wasn't going to change anything. Worrying wasn't going to fix anything. There was nothing I could do about the flood now.

I chose the higher route. I went upstairs and prayed. It could have been worse. I was lucky I was home. I gave thanks for the people that had come to help and everything else I had to be grateful for. I showered, did my hair, and got all dolled up. I went out and celebrated the birthday of an acquaintance like nothing had happened. I had promised myself that 2014 was going to be a better year than the year before and it looked like it was going to be a challenge. I wasn't about to give in not even 24 hours into the year. I was determined not to let the day's events ruin my plan for the next 364 days. I celebrated like it was New Year's Eve and then some!

The flood was a symbol of what was in store for the remainder of the year. The year 2014 has been filled with a waterfall of blessings. My life has been flooded with things to be grateful for. I have had my share of struggles, but the positives outweigh the negatives. It is what I have chosen to do in the bad times and how I react that have attracted happiness.

Consider this: do you enjoy being around people that are positive, enthusiastic about life, and happy? Of course you do. They make us feel good. Those same people may have just as much problems as the negative, unhappy person wallowing in pity. It's how they choose to react to life and their positive outlook that others are attracted to and enjoy being around.

Opportunities and encouragement come from others. So what happens when people enjoy being around you? You get more opportunities and encouragement. A life filled with opportunity and encouragement attracts more and more opportunity and encouragement. Success is inevitable with an overflow of opportunity and encouragement. "My cup runneth over" (Psalm 23:5). That's abundance!

God doesn't love the positive person any more than the negative person. Always be grateful for your life as things could be worse. Focus on the positive and attract more positive. The exact opposite is also true. If you focus on the negatives, you attract more of that into your world. No one wants to be around someone who is always negative, complains, and is difficult to get along with. That person repels others and they receive less encouragement and fewer opportunities. You can only imagine what happens to a life without encouragement and opportunities.

Despite my past of hurts and failed relationships, I have learned to acknowledge my part in those situations. No one deserves to be hurt. The old me did a lot more complaining than I realized. I wasn't as grateful as I could have been. I contributed to my mess with my reaction to the actions of others. I paid a hefty price. Today I share my mistakes to prevent others from making those same mistakes. It is my message today. How can your past help someone else's future?

Use the gifts you have been blessed with and share them with others. The seeds you sow today affect the harvest that you receive tomorrow. Sow a good seed and you receive good harvest. Sow a bad seed and you will reap bad harvest. You can call it karma, circle of life, law of attraction, call it whatever you choose. Just be mindful of what you put out into the universe.

When I share my divorce story with others they often ask how I am still able to wish my former husband well. It was a process. It was part of my healing. I could be bitter but that only affects me and those around me. I don't care for the negative energy. Today I genuinely wish him well in life. He has to deal with his own karma; that's not on me. He has to answer to God at the end of the day for how he handled the situation. He was raised Muslim so call him Allah if you prefer, either way he has to deal with a higher being.

His take on the entire situation may be different. That is purely due to perspective. We may never see eye-to-eye on what happened during the divorce, but I'm content with that. A fish and a bird both see the world in an entirely different light. It is based on their perspective. They will never have the same perspective, but if they understand that both views and opinions are based on their knowledge/angle, they can attempt to see where the other is coming from and respect the other's perspective.

My mess was my life, but my message from the divorce came by how I dealt with the events that occurred. I was fully dependent on an older man for years. I didn't have to work or worry about how a bill was going to be paid. The refrigerator was stocked with groceries all the time. When I chose to work, it was to buy things to make the home look pretty or clothes for my children and shoes for myself. I was living a spoiled life with rose-colored glasses on. I had it pretty good according to some. I had no concept of how the average person lived or the struggles they had.

I didn't expect that to end. I wasn't prepared for my lifestyle to change. When the relationship ended, I wasn't as independent as I am today. When I ended the relationship I didn't expect him to walk out with both hands in the air leaving us to survive alone. I felt like I was pushed out of a plane with no parachute. As I was falling fast and gravity was pulling me to smash my face against the concrete, my survival skills kicked in—that first level of awareness, that animal instinct of fight or flight, and that notion to react versus respond. As I was falling, I thought about my kids and how this would break them unless I did something quickly. The more I looked at their faces and saw fear in their eyes, the more I knew I had to be strong. I spread my wings and began to glide until I landed softly on my feet.

I had no time to feel sorry for myself. I had a mess to clean up. I had to learn things quickly without a security blanket to catch me if I slipped. Understanding how to handle stress took time; it took many trips to the hospital with blinding migraines. Setback after setback I had to gain experience in coping with disappointment. I had no idea what it was to lack for anything financially. I had to learn how to survive on my own with three dependents.

Think about leaving a child alone in the wild with no survival skills. To me the thought is terrifying because that was how I felt until I acquired the skills to survive. I learned them by doing, by acting, and by experiencing. That hard time built me up to the strong woman I am today. I had two choices to make as I was falling. I could continue to fall and when I hit rock bottom, be the victim. I chose instead to be victorious and fight like my life depended on it.

I won that fight. You can't use an egg until it is cracked open. I landed on my feet and I'm still standing. In the process I got acquainted with life, enjoying the blessings that came out of my lessons. My life is now enriched with truer friendships, deeper bonds, beautiful connections, and more support than I had when I was married. I feel dependent and proud of myself for the accomplishments whether they are small, medium, or large.

You never really know your partner until you divorce them, even when you think you know them better than they know themselves. That can be taken as a positive or a negative. The entire divorce process taught me a lot about myself, my ex, and those around me. I was able to see how cold some people really are and just how amazing and underestimated others were. Crisis doesn't change you; it brings out who you really are. The process taught me to be more open to the perspectives of others.

When I am attempting to help others, I try to understand their perspective and how I can assist from their angle. What part of my mess will be a good message for them? What message will fit best with where they are in life? What do I want to accomplish when sharing with them? And how much detail do they deserve to hear?

My sister, before she passed away, once wrote, "What you are going through is not an attack. What you are going through is heaven's birthing contractions and you are getting ready to be delivered. Your tears mean that the water has broken. A pearl comes from hardship. We've all been through something. But God doesn't waste any experience. Every person and family has a womb to birth some things. Be not dismayed or sad when you are rejected. Rejection is not a sign that there is something wrong with you. Rejection is a divine announcement that the person who rejected you no longer has the capacity for your greatness. Stop crying; you are blessed. This is not the time to give up; push. You're not crazy...you're pregnant by God and about to deliver....God is so good!"

She surely had a way with making me feel like my struggles were for a purpose. She had a gift of putting a positive spin on my most challenging moments. She was blessed with the ability to pull others out of their rough patches and use that experience to help inspire others. I have taken on that task to honour her now that she is no longer here on earth.

God can take your mess and turn it into a beautiful message. A touching quote I see floating around often on the Internet that reminds me of my sister's words is, "Only God can turn a MESS into a MESSage, a TEST into a TESTimony, a TRIal into a TRIumph, a VICTim into a VICTory. God is good...all the time!"

Chapter 11

- BEING A SINGLE MOTHER -

Being a mother requires sacrifice. Being a single mother feels like the ultimate sacrifice. My pastor had once said, "Faith pushes out sacrifice. The level of your sacrifice shows your faith. Sacrificial people don't go around broadcasting it." What I do for my children isn't easy, but I don't go around complaining/bragging about it. I brought them into this world and feel it is my responsibility to give them the best that I can.

I chose to bring my children into this world; they did not ask to be here. They do not owe me anything. It is my job to make sure they do not regret my decision. Love, security, and happiness are my debt to them. Providing these necessities squares the deal. My job is to make each child feel special and precious.

As women, we may have many jobs in our lifetime, but being a single mother is one of the most rewarding yet the most demanding job we may ever have. There will be times that we get overwhelmed and feel we are being pulled in a hundred different directions at once. There are times that we feel 24 hours aren't enough to accomplish the chores, parental duties, and other life responsibilities on our plates.

There are times I wonder to myself how I manage, but I know it's only by God's grace. There are women with husbands and overly supportive families that can't handle the demands of being a parent and I do it solo. Being a single parent is difficult but it is manageable. When I feel overwhelmed, I think about all the strong single mothers I observed growing up. My mother, sister, aunts, neighbours, and even celebrities who have gracefully raised children on their own and made so many life sacrifices that I have to honour them.

There is a list of well-known people who have been raised by single mothers and gone on to do great things in the world despite the number of adults still showing signs of being damaged from divorce. Children of divorce suffer their own hurt and misplaced feelings, and if the parents are not careful they, bring up emotionally injured adults. I'm very aware of this and nurture the emotional needs of my children. Possibly at times over-compensating and being over-affectionate, but I never want them to not feel loved.

Motherhood for me has to be the ultimate job, my greatest assignment. The reward of watching my children grow towards independence, become their own individuals with views and opinions is far greater than the financial compensation I will ever receive from any other job. Some mothers are too caught up in the everyday hustle of trying to get through a work day, meeting the demands of their children, and maintaining a home to stop and acknowledge the true value of the work they are doing in this world. There is such significance in our job as a nurturer, caregiver, friend, and teacher. There are so many levels to the position we carry that they are often taken for granted in the daily bustle.

Providing for three dependents, financially, can be challenging, but balance is needed to ensure that all their needs are being met. From the moment I had my first child, I established that I was a parent who worked to live and provide for my family. I would never be the kind of person who lives to work and revolves their life around work. My family comes first and work is balanced around that. I am a full-time mother, a mompreneur. All children require time devoted to them for reading, talking, play, homework, and bonding. They require our attention just as much as they require the necessities of life that we work so hard to provide.

For some women, the challenge is finding a job or career that allows the balance needed to be the sole provider and caregiver for her child/children. When I only had two children and was working, attending school, and attempting to be a good mother, my children lost out the most; hence, my decision to be self-employed after the divorce. It allowed me the flexibility to juggle my schedule as a mother and to be there for my children, giving me the ability to be present for the moments I can never get back.

There are companies out there today that accommodate childcare or have shifts that make getting to daycare in time easier. I much prefer building my work around my children so I'm able to play a more active role in their day-to-day. I don't have to miss a track meet, awards ceremony, or even the opportunity to volunteer. Those moments are very important to me and I know they are even more important to my children.

Growing up my mother had quite the load working to be the sole provider for three children and her parents. She wasn't able to balance being there for her kids on weekdays with her work schedule. She missed every track meet, every awards ceremony, and was never able to volunteer. I never blamed her for that, but it didn't make the pain any less. I don't ever want my kids to feel that. Since being in real estate there have been opportunities to make money, but I chose to put my kids first, remembering what it had been like for myself.

As much as I was able to learn from my mother growing up, I want my children to learn from me. I observed my mother throughout life and that has molded me into who I am today. I was never very good at doing what she told me to do but picked up habits very quickly. Now that I have children of my own, I understand very well how the cycle works. It is my job to teach my children life skills, but simply telling them what to do isn't teaching them anything.

Knowing how our practices and habits affect the little people watching us, we need to be mindful of what lessons we want them to learn. All of my actions are thought out as to how they will affect my children in the near or distant future. My practices around my faith, my relationships with people, how I handle money, are all done with them in consideration. We need to lead by example, show them, guide their steps as they mimic us, but allow them the freedom to learn by experience on the way. Rather than spoon-feed them information, we need to show them how to obtain that knowledge on their own. Give a man a fish and you feed him for a day; teach him how to fish and you feed him for life.

As much as we are the teachers, we must also be open to being students. Our children are often the best teachers. A mother that feels she has nothing to learn from her child is fooling herself. A child has numerous skills that we lack or have lost and could use a reminder on. My children have the ability to teach me daily. Whether it is patience, or how to live in the moment, to get over disappointment quickly, or to make decisions quicker, they have skills that we lack. It changes our relationship with them when we realize the exchange of knowledge.

I've found being a single mother has made me a little uptight at times and my children are the greatest at softening me up. My obsessive compulsive ways of keeping everything in order and on schedule is innocently and at times purposely toyed with by them. They teach me so much about life and make me want to stop to enjoy it.

Being a single mother has made me a more rounded individual. It's reminded me that it isn't ever always about me. If I had a partner to share the load, I may possibly have room to be self-centered but I don't, so I'm not. It is difficult to have ME time, but it is necessary so I make the effort. Single motherhood is extremely hard work so making time for me is a priority. We carry the workload of two people. Going to the gym in the morning/night, getting my hair and nails done regularly, and making time to enjoy the company of other adults are ways that I recharge.

Even as single parents, there are times we expect the other parent to participate. I used to get worked up when my children's father didn't show effort or want to be involved in things I felt were fatherly duties. It took growth on my part to realize that I can't control anyone but myself. Expecting was setting me up for disappointment. In my journey of growth, I no longer expect anything. When my children's father decides to take part, it's a bonus. It isn't fair that I have to physically and financially do the majority of the work, but depending on the help and not receiving it was too stressful. I no longer lose sleep over things I can't control. I focus on being the best mother possible. My childhood sweetheart has made efforts to be a better father as the girls get older, and for that I'm grateful.

The pressures of being a single mother can cause you to lose your cool at times, but yelling and screaming at the kids doesn't help them or you. How can we teach our children anything if we ourselves haven't learned how to be patient? The moments when our children make us frustrated or upset are usually the times when they need us the most. We lose our cool by some lack of ability or understanding on their part, missing the opportunity to help them learn. As humans we feel we are the most sophisticated, yet lack the basic skill of patience the animals and plants seem to have in abundance. Birds migrate in the winter, plants wait for spring to bud, yet as people we haven't mastered this skill.

I was angry during the divorce and yelled at my kids more often than I care to admit. I was furious all the time. I was called out by a close friend, and I had to evaluate my coping mechanisms. I found other things to help handle the pressure of having to be "on" all the time.

Two-parent homes have the luxury of passing the responsibility back and forth. Two-parent homes allow for some sort of trade-off when a parent comes in from work. As a single parent the heat is always on and losing your cool is bound to happen. When my emotions are boiling over and I feel like yelling at my kids for a mess or something they shouldn't have done, I walk away for a ten-second count or I go to my room to calm down until those feelings subside.

Children have two parents because they need two parents. A mother cannot be everything a child needs, and only ignorance will allow a woman to feel that way. Those that try to do it all achieve less than those that recognize their own limits. Some people are better than others at being gentle, affectionate, understanding, exciting, firm, patient, physically active, mentally stimulating, and all the other qualities a child needs in a parent to flourish.

It is not our job to be all things nor is that a realistic expectation of ourselves. If we believe unrealistic things, we set ourselves up for failure. All of these qualities may not even be fulfilled between both parents. It is merely our job as mothers to ensure that our children have access to these attributes from somewhere.

We have to live in the moment or else we miss out on enjoyment. In this time of technology, we are so busy staring at the small screen of our phones and smart gadgets that we don't enjoy the people and scenery in front of us. As the old saying goes, "Stop and smell the roses." Sometimes we need to slow down and absorb our surroundings. There is so much beauty to see in this world if we take the time to acknowledge it.

I tend to get caught up in the fast lane most times and life has to stop me in my tracks to get my attention. It's usually in the form of one of my children, as nothing else takes precedence.

Being a realtor, I'm always on the go. I woke up on Mother's Day morning ready for the one day a week that I actually take off. I got out of bed to get ready for church with the kids and was excited that my brother and I were taking my mother to lunch. My son walked into my room with fluid-filled bumps all over his face. He had chickenpox.

At first I was upset, thinking my Mother's Day was ruined, my week would have to be rescheduled, my....., my....., etc. By midday I was over it and realized I was only thinking about the negative result on my end goals and how it affected me. Not only was this a time for me to relax and slow down, but my son needed some TLC and mommy time that didn't include his siblings.

The remainder of the day consisted of us bonding. We cuddled in bed, we read a few books, we talked about the things that interested him, and we watched a little television. My Sundays are usually reserved for church and family, but it became my SONday. We needed that time for us. Not only did I realize the need to slow down but also my son enjoyed it more than anything. It was a nice distraction from his chickenpox.

That afternoon I moved all appointments to the following week. I had to cancel a few things that couldn't be rescheduled, but my son needed me. As the week went on, I appreciated more and more the slower pace life and began to see the beauty all around me. The weather outside was nice and warm, so during our quarantine we would go for walks and bike rides while the neighbourhood was at school or work.

My son has been a nature lover since birth and educated me on the different species of birds. We enjoyed watching Blue Jays, Cardinals, Humming Birds, Robins, etc. We watched squirrels play, dogs walk, and cats roam. We soaked up the sun while we exercised on our bike rides and walks all week. It was beautiful. We literally stopped to smell the roses.

The following week, when I returned to my workweek, I was fine. I picked up where I let off before my "staycation." I stopped to enjoy my son. I lived in that very moment and loved it! The beauty in my surroundings was fully appreciated. I even noticed that my son was growing up right in front of me with his advanced conversations. Seeing him every day, I failed to realize he wasn't my baby anymore but an intelligent young boy that was sprouting up before my eyes. I was so busy getting through each day that I missed taking a moment to enjoy the little things along the way. When did he become so smart?

Live in the moment and enjoy your children. Once they learn new skills or acquire new talents, they are never the same again. They grow so quickly that we often forget to enjoy them in the stage they are currently in. The once small child rapidly becomes this large person with his or her own needs and wants.

Create an environment of acceptance as the children grow. Allow them to evolve on their own into who they were meant to be. I give my children the space and freedom to be individuals. All three are very different and I embrace it. I don't like disappointment, so I don't hold heavy expectations over my children. I don't expect them to live up to my interests or ambitions. I'm not trying to create minions or copies of myself. They wouldn't be individuals in that case.

I allow my children to have a voice, but they must be respectful. I want them to learn from a young age that their opinions matter. We have open conversations and I ask their opinion. I build a connection with them in this manner and it allows for open dialogue. They feel more comfortable coming to me with issues that they face at school, with friends, or even their father. Our communication goes both ways. I have found when I communicate with them what is happening or going to happen, they behave and cooperate much easier.

My children are all very intelligent. I haven't dated much since the divorce and I'm sure my kids notice there isn't a man around, but I make that sacrifice for them. I didn't like anyone my mother dated growing up. I remember the awkward feeling of pretending to like them. I don't want just any man around my kids unless I feel they will be more of a permanent fixture in my life. They don't need to be subjected to seeing different men unless they are platonic friendships.

Children with single mothers should be exposed to positive male role models. They need to see and be told about great men so that it doesn't destroy their perception of men. My children regularly see their godfather, who is a wonderful example of a male role model. If the father is not present, it is very important that children see examples of how a good man behaves and treats women. Seek out positive models for them. I have many brothers but they don't live in a close enough proximity to be that figure to the children. My father is a loving and helpful example but does not live in the country. My son was paired with the school's principal during a time when I wasn't able to provide one.

Parenting children with love versus fear allows them to respect you. Not having a man around as a single parent doesn't mean we need to take on the masculine trait of instilling fear into our children. Parenting with love will get more out of a child than fear. When a child fears you, they do not do things from a good place and they tend to act out or shut down and you lose respect and trust.

As a single mother, I feel it is important to provide a spiritual foundation for my children. It is my responsibility to set the stage for their future. By instilling values and acknowledging a higher being, I'm laying the foundation for my children. They are not given an option if they want to attend church with me on Sundays. If they decide when they are older that they do not want to, I have at least introduced them to the importance of spirituality and God's house. Even if they are not paying attention to the entire service, the word is being placed into their subconscious. The practices in the environment are now habitual.

Teaching kids faith and allowing them to believe in the unseen isn't actually difficult at all. It is children that have the most faith in possibility that have the greatest imagination. It is only as they get older and life experience dulls these treasures that they lose sight of these golden abilities. Helping to keep that alive is setting them up for a great future. It builds a mindset of endless possibilities and opens the subconscious to the gift of opportunities that are waiting to be seen.

A small child cannot tell the difference between fact and fairy tale. Adults ruin this by trying to teach them the difference instead of helping them to inhabit this charm where the magic happens. We read our children fairy tales and feed the imagination then turn around and destroy it by forcing on them to be realistic and live in conformity the second they are old enough to understand. We are their very first teachers of believing in the unknown. We contribute to whether or not they live in faith or fear.

One thing most single mothers do is forget to congratulate themselves. It is rare that someone else is going to say, "You're doing a great job on your own." That pat on the back that you may be looking for may not come. It's hard work and feeling appreciated starts with acknowledging the hard work put in. I congratulate myself every time I place a meal on the table and my kids say, "Thank you mommy," or when my kids come home from school with good grades or when someone says, "Your kids are so well behaved." I did that, and I did it alone.

There is no greater gift we can give our children than their childhood. If you take away from their first years you deprive their entire life. Stimulating a child's mind and adding to who they can be in the future is worth more than all the money in the world. Mental stimulation is essential. As single parents, we must feed the mind of our children. They are like a plant; without water they do not grow. They need mental stimulation to grow. Provide variety and newness in their lives. These elements will allow them to flourish.

Today is called the present for a reason. It's a gift. Enjoy it. Tomorrow is promised to no one and yesterday is gone. Learn from your past, prepare for the future, but most of all live in the moment. Enjoy today and be grateful for the opportunity, as there are many that did not wake this morning and others that will not see the light of day tomorrow. Everything that happens is for a reason so allow life to happen, the good and the bad. Life doesn't happen to you, it happens for you. Find the beauty in all of it.

As a single parent, I do twice the amount of work and have twice the amount of stress, but that comes with two times the amount of rewards—twice the amount of love from my children.

Chapter 12

- MONEY AND BUSINESS -

What most of the population fails to understand about money is that it is available to us all, but it begins with our feelings towards it. Like everything else in this world, mindset plays a tremendous role in earning money and success in business. The conditioning of the mind (paradigm) affects our success and our ability to earn money.

We all have the same 24 hours in a day. We are all brought into this world through the same process, and we will all be reduced to the same thing at the end of the day. The difference between the wealthy successful people in this world and those that struggle in life is the mindset and understanding of how things work. Knowledge and awareness are key. We operate in frequency and need to get on the money frequency to attract money-earning opportunities into our lives. "And my God shall supply every need of yours according to his riches in the glory in Christ Jesus" (Philippians 4:19).

There are no hand-outs in life. There is no such thing as something for nothing. Everything has some form of cost, even if it isn't monetary. Money is compensation for the service we provide to others. Money isn't a reward until we earn plenty of it. Motivation has to be the reward. Money is meant for two things on this earth. One is to make us comfortable. It allows us to buy the things we like and to live a comfortable life. Two is to extend it to help others. Give to those in need and support the less fortunate. When we have a better understanding of money, we are not so selfish with it. Money is a servant and we are the masters, not the other way around.

What are your current thoughts about money? Do you hoarder it hoping to someday be rich? Do you use it to help others? Do you live in a scarcity frame of mind thinking that it will soon end and you won't have enough to survive? Do you sow seeds into charities or a place of worship? "Every man according as he purposeth in his heart, [so let him give]; not grudgingly, or of necessity: for God loveth a cheerful giver" (2 Corinthians 9:7).

What you are currently earning today as income doesn't matter nor does your level of education in terms of what you can earn in the near future. Riches are available to every one of us; you just have to be ready for it and be determined to receive the blessings. The first time I was given the pleasure of listening to Bob Proctor speak in person, I was shocked to hear that this multimillionaire only had two weeks of high school. Bill Gates, Steve Jobs, and Mark Zuckerberg also dropped out of school but went on to be extremely successful. These men all had passion, determination, perseverance, and consistency. Most importantly they had the mindset needed to succeed.

These great men are part of the three percent of the population earning 97 percent of the money in this world and making things happen. I wanted to be a part of that but wasn't exactly sure how. I was a part of the 97 percent of the population living an average life per se mixing with other unsuccessful people. I had been told that it starts in the mind. The very first step is in your desire. When I made the effort to change my life and my mindset, it set the stage for the opportunities that followed.

I shifted to a new paradigm when I made the decision to do something about my situation. No one can do that for you. That is something that you have to do on your own. I changed what I thought about money and I changed what I did with it. I heard Bob Proctor say, "People don't buy what they want; they buy what they can afford." I was thinking about money in terms of a negative state instead of in the positive state. I acquired the knowledge of focusing on positive wealth and not debt. As I had said previously, we attract what we focus on.

As much as I hated to admit it, I was not living with the mindset to ever be wealthy financially. I was rich in relationships and love, but my finances were not overflowing. I was conditioned to think about money by what I had been taught growing up, what I had learned from my parents. School certainly didn't teach me anything about money other than how to count it.

I had to unlearn everything I was taught in the past about money and become a complete sponge to knowledge from the people that had a lot of it. I was tired of listening to other struggling people telling me what I should be doing with my money, where I should invest it, or judging what I chose to spend my money on. It wasn't until I began to spend more time with wealthy successful people that I was able to become intentional with my thoughts about money and success. The architect of the universe created me with a divine purpose in mind, it was time to comprehend that and live the life that was designed for me.

I chose a few heavy hitters. We don't need to be surrounded by too many people at once. These successful people that I surrounded myself with had money but were very giving and generous. These individuals were willing to share their knowledge and experience. They are some of the most humble people I have ever had the pleasure of meeting. What I admired most was that they all had a charity with which they shared their wealth.

These extremely successful people taught me that there are things that I am going to have to do that others won't to get where I want to go. I agreed to be open-minded as long as it didn't compromise my faith and values. They have shown me that in order to be successful I will have to do things that others are not willing to do. I will have to make quick decisions, take risks, be mocked, and have a mass of people that may not agree with what I do. If I want to succeed, I will have to be illogical, take risks, and get comfortable with being uncomfortable.

Most people don't have a money problem; they have a perception problem. Making money and being successful have nothing to do with your perception and everything to do with your performance. Most people want to have lots of money but don't want to do the work. Most people feel they have to trade time for money. In fact, time has nothing to do with the amount of money you earn. We all have the same 24 hours in a day and no one person has any more potential than the next. It's all in your actions. Your performance and the steps you take towards goals. If God brought you to it, he will bring you through it.

When the average person wants to earn more income, he or she adds more shifts at work and spends more hours of the day. Some will even get a second job and trade more of their time hoping to make enough money to cover their expenses. This isn't going to make you successful. This just makes you 97 percent of the population living in mediocrity. I refuse to live my life this way.

There are those that want the entrepreneurial life and choose to purchase a franchise and start their business that way. This route requires money to get started and the return isn't immediate. The pressure of managing employees, maintaining a property, carrying a lease, and the risk of losing my initial investment doesn't appeal to me either.

My success has come from partnering. I have gained plenty by partnering with other like-minded people. For real estate, I have partnered with other agents to leverage our abilities and skill sets. We are able to exchange services in business, and there is little to no training required due to the same credentials required for our profession. For clients, I have partnered with an event planner, a professional photographer, a caterer, and a mobile spa that have brand credibility to provide complimentary house warming parties to my buyer clients. The benefits of having multiple companies promoting your business and the word of mouth from all attendees build an audience greater than traditional marketing.

Since partnering with multimillionaires like the Proctor family to build residual income, I have seen the advantage of partnership with people that have huge brand credibility. Well-known companies use celebrity endorsements to sell a product. I have access to Bob Proctor and his lovely wife, Linda, and daughter, Colleen, who have become my mentors. They have spent years building their brands and credibility and would not put that at risk. When others see who I'm working with and the network I'm connected to, it builds my credibility.

Leveraging all of our efforts as a team not only makes the workload pressure less, but it also has been a fun learning experience. The skills I am learning from the team are applicable to my entire life. They are teaching me to be a better leader, face my fears, embrace my faith, be a giving problem solver, and focus on the positives. All of this is by following systems. Systems don't fail; people do. That alone is life-changing.

Being successful takes a team. If you ask any successful person how they got to where they are, they'll tell you that they didn't do it alone. They had help. They were backed by a handful of others that supported their vision. You can be in business by yourself, but you can't do it alone. "The collective wisdom of independent ignorance doesn't work." I remember hearing Bob Proctor say those words the first time I heard him speak in person. He spoke to me and about 30 others in a hotel meeting room.

Remove hierarchy and competition and learn to work with others. You can't be a master at everything. You have to leverage the skills and gifts of others. Every one of us has a different level of skill. Each member of your team may have mastered an area that you cannot or just don't want to. Don't try to be a jack of all trades, master of none. Research shows that we learn effectively from each other. Teams are more progressive than individuals when working on complex projects.

There is power in numbers. If you try to lift a heavy object with your pinky finger you will fail; the weight may even hurt the finger. If you try to lift an object with two fingers you may not have any success either. If you combine the power of all five fingers on a hand or the power of ten fingers, you will lift the object with much ease. When you make use of all members of the team and distribute the weight, it doesn't seem to weigh down one person.

Becoming a part of the business team and working directly with the Proctor family has given goal setting an entire new meaning. Our success goals cause us to reach and stretch for greatness. All that I was reaching for before wasn't sufficient. I have been taught how to strive for bigger goals, ones that scare me. I was taught in the past to set goals that are attainable so I don't feel as if they are out of reach. In the past I was trained to set goals that I see myself attaining. This learned behaviour was short-changing my potential.

We all have infinite potential. When we set proper goals, we should not know how we are going to achieve them until we do. The goal should be so large that we have no idea how we are ever going to achieve it. It should be specific, written to your present self from a future date in a positive tone. Even if you are unable to reach that goal by the date set, you have pushed yourself and worked towards it, stretched past where you thought you could have in order to try and reach that goal. You're not going after the goal to reach the goal; it's to reach and grow. You haven't limited yourself to a refined goal. You will then see what potential you really have.

As long as your focus is on the goal, all that you require to attain it will attract to you. Wherever your energy goes, that is what manifests in your life. Everything in the universe operates by law. There will be a point as you are working towards your goals that you will feel like quitting. There will be moments of discomfort or maybe even anxiety. The butterflies are normal; it's training them to fly into formation that affects your end result. If you are not prepared to deal with the discomfort, then chances are you will stay right where you are in life. Comfort zones don't breed change.

Wealth comes from definite demand by definite precision. There is a system. It is a reward for service. Be of service to others. Spend time with people that are making lots of money and follow their systems and help others. If we are a product of the books we read and the people we associate with, then you can only gain from surrounding yourself with successful individuals that know how to earn and manage money. We don't have to accept the conventional gradual progress of success. We have the ability to skip levels, to make quantum leaps, to multiply as opposed to add. It's all connected to the mindset you have, the people you surround yourself with, and the effort you put in.

Most wealthy successful people in this world have money coming in from more than one place. They don't have all their eggs in one basket. If something like a job loss or injury happened, they would still have income coming in. We need to be smart about our income and money management. I learned this lesson the hard way. When my sister passed away, and I was an emotional, mental wreck, I could not work. I wasn't answering calls or even checking e-mails.

What happened to my income? It stopped. Real estate was my only source of income at that time. I made a vow to myself that I wouldn't be in that position again. Since then, I have been open to opportunities that provide multiple sources of income. My time is limited as I am devoted to my children and I make no exception to missing church, but as I mentioned before, you don't have to trade time for money.

Make your money work hard for you, don't overwork yourself for money. A single income as a single mother of three was not enough to provide for my family, and if I had a nine-to-five my struggle may have been much more difficult. I now have multiple sources of income that align with my brand of helping others and don't require my presence to do so.

Writing this book is proof of that. I'm earning money continually off of efforts put in one time. I wrote the material and will earn income off of royalties when a book is purchased. That is the beauty of residual income. There are musicians that have passed away and their estate is making more money than when they were alive off of royalties from the work they had done at one time. They are not here on this earth now to trade time, but the money is still coming in.

If it is done the right way, network marketing is another form of residual income that can pay full-time based on part-time hours. If you are running around pushing product, you will not succeed as you are trading time for a small percentage of income. If you build a network of people that product moves through, you will have a higher success rate. Your income grows as your team grows.

I had many people over the years approach me about being part of multi-level marketing over the years and never once did it appeal to me. I had no interest in doing product parties in living rooms or trying to convince anyone to buy anything. Even as a real estate agent, I don't force my clients to purchase a home. That's possibly the largest purchase they will ever make in their lives, and I couldn't sleep at night if they felt pressured to buy a home and regretted it later.

When I met Linda Proctor and realized she had become a multimillionaire through network marketing by not pushing product but by simply building a network of people that used the product, a lightbulb went off in my head. I could earn income doing something I was already doing for free! I connect with people and build relationships on a daily basis through real estate, social media, and just being out and about. If I simply applied what Linda Proctor was willing to teach me, I could improve the lives of those around me that saw the vision and improve my own life at the same time.

If I could help people become healthier by consuming clinically studied liquid vitamins and possibly make more money than they made doing their full-time job without them having to quit, I could sleep at night with a clean heart. They would also benefit from the mentorship of the Proctors that is an opportunity of a lifetime. I was improving their lives in more ways than one.

I'm providing a service: the formula to attracting money. I'm providing an opportunity to increase their finances and build for retirement, something not available to everyone. I'm offering mentorship to build their skill set, which cost them nothing but has endless value. I'm bringing awareness to their health and giving them the ability to increase their energy and lose weight. What better way to make a living than helping improve the lives of others? "For where your treasure is, there will your heart be also" (Luke 12:34).

Chapter 13

- GIVE THANKS BY GIVING -

Give as you've never given before. Give your time, give your knowledge, give your money to those less fortunate. Give thanks by giving has become a motto I live by. It has brightened up my life and brought me joy in many ways through giving back. You don't have to be rich or have a lot in order to give. What you give doesn't have to be financial in order to have value. What you give doesn't have to be much in order to make a difference.

I'm a firm believer in giving unselfishly. There is great joy in giving and being of help and service to others. Being able to bless another is where you will find great joy and pleasure. It comes back to you. Each time you are blessed, pay it forward and bless another. "He that withholdeth corn, the people shall curse him; But blessing shall be upon the head of him that selleth it" (Proverbs 11:26).

When I was growing up, I watched my single mother, who worked two jobs at times to provide for her children, open our home to give others shelter. She would provide food, clothing, and time to those that were in need. She never complained or expected anything in return. Even when someone didn't show gratitude or took advantage of her kindness, she would still extend her hands to the next person that needed it.

As I grew older and began paying attention to the world, I realized how much a small gesture meant to those I would help. Doing my daily good deed for a stranger became a simple habit. Paying it forward every time someone did something kind for me just felt like the right thing to do. I've come to realize now that helping others has many rewards in life. "The wicked borroweth, and payeth not again; But the righteous dealeth graciously, and giveth" (Psalm 37:21).

There is much talk all over the Bible of sowing and reaping. You sow good seeds, you reap good harvest. You sow bad seeds, you reap bad harvest. We reap whatever we sow. If you want to benefit from a good harvest, you must produce it. If you want more out of life, give more. If you want more time, love, or money, you must first give more time, love, or money. This can't be done in a selfish manner though. There is a process. It requires work and it has to be done for the right reasons and it must be genuine.

Volunteering

Volunteering my time cost nothing but has so much value. When I make the choice to invest my time into my community, I never have an expectation of what I'm going to receive out of it. Yet I always leave feeling filled. My heart filled with love. My mind filled with memories. My spirit filled with joy. The value on that kind of fulfilment is priceless. There is no amount of money in the world that equates to improving, changing, and affecting lives for the better.

If my schedule permits and I hear of an opportunity to volunteer, I'm in! In November 2013, there was a typhoon in the Philippines. A friend of mine was part of a team hosting a fundraiser to raise funds to send the Red Cross that was matching donations. They asked for assistance in any way on social media. At the time I was saving up to buy my kids' presents for Christmas and I didn't have a lot of money coming in from work that month. I wasn't in the greatest position to give a financial contribution that I would have been pleased with.

I wanted to help, so I offered my time. What does a few hours of one evening cost me? I showed up with no idea what I would be doing, but I was there to help in any way possible that would raise funds for the victims of the natural disaster. I not only found pleasure in assisting with the event, but I made connections that night. I made new friends while I volunteered, and my existing friends from the Filipino community were touched that I wanted to help. "Give her of the fruit of her hands; And let her works praise her in the gates" (Proverbs 31:31).

Volunteering benefits you, your family, the community, and the world. It makes your community a better place and connects you to the people in it. It gives you the opportunity to practice and develop your social skills. It allows you to network and make new friends and business contacts. Giving back gives a sense of pride and identity. It's also a good way to brand your business and let people know what matters to you. Be a citizen of God and give to the world.

Random acts of kindness

Going the extra step to make a family member or friend feel good is another way I enjoy giving. Random gifts and cards when they least expect it can make their day or even week. A gift to say, "I'm grateful to have you in my life" means more to me as the giver than it may mean to the receiver. Actually paying attention when they speak can give clues to the little things that matter to them. Using those clues, I surprise them with small things that light up their face to show my appreciation.

I was at a friend's gathering at her home when she mentioned during a conversation with a group of people that she always wanted balloons for her birthday. The day arrived and she had no plans and was home for the day. I was busy with clients and appointments that day and didn't have the time to spend with her. I stopped at the closest party store to her home, picked a bunch of balloons in her favourite colours, and had them blown up. I sent her a quick text message to ask permission to stop by for a second and showed up with the bulk of balloons in hand.

The look on her face was priceless and heartwarming. She felt special and heard. I made her day. She was so happy she posted a picture of her birthday balloons on social media. I had no idea how much it would mean to her when I decided to surprise her, but I knew for myself that the gesture was worth a try. It cost me no more than 10 minutes and 10 dollars. The value of the memory and the feeling isn't one that can be calculated, but it holds weight. "And in your godliness brotherly kindness; and in your brotherly kindness love" (2 Peter 1:7).

I enjoy giving that feeling to strangers also. I like to grab a cappuccino on Sunday mornings on my way to church. I always go into the drive-thru as I'm usually in a rush to get to service. I pay for the order of the person behind me. What is a couple of dollars to make another person's day? That kind gesture could change their perception of people altogether. Give them a reason to be a better person. Who knows...I'm sowing a seed into their life.

Sponsorship

Sponsoring charity events is another way that I give back. Attaching my brand to a charity event that I care about helps to show my support both financially and physically. I enjoy bringing awareness to the cause in front of an audience that may not have otherwise been aware. It assists in the marketing of the charity event and I'm able to have my peers help promote what I am involved in to give the charity greater exposure and hopefully raise more funds. It reaches out to all demographics and creates an environment with endless boundaries. Helping in this form can have a great impact on all parties involved.

I always thought that is was only big brands that sponsored teams and events, but I learned a few years ago that anyone can. When I was fresh in my field as a realtor, I didn't even have a logo and began sponsoring events. I was asked by a friend if I would like to sponsor a charity event being put on to raise funds for a women's shelter. I didn't care for the recognition; I wanted to help and the opportunity was there. It was a busy time of year and I wasn't able to volunteer. It was a weeknight and I was volunteering my time the following day for another large event.

I gladly sent the funds to help with the event. At the time I didn't know much about the shelter they were supporting, but I knew it provided assistance to women in need. I happened to be leaving church one Sunday and a wonderful woman I had become acquainted with approached me. She was super excited and wanted to share a story with me. She had seen on social media that I was sponsoring an event that was giving all proceeds to a women's shelter in her area. She had once relied on that shelter for assistance during a rough patch in her life. She was so grateful for what they were able to do for her and her children that it gave me a feeling of such humility. It was helping closer to home than I had expected.

The following year when I was asked if I would sponsor the event once again, without hesitation I said yes. The events were touching lives. Not only did the shelter have the funds to help the women and their families in the community, but the event itself was fulfilling to those that attended. The givers came together to give thanks and support the less fortunate.

The funds used to sponsor an event help make things happen. There are costs involved in having an event and when you are trying to raise funds you want to eliminate the amount of costs and have the funds raised go towards helping where it is needed most: the cause.

As an individual and/or a company, we have influence over others. Leverage your influence and network into supporting the cause and use your power to have others do something with you. As a sponsor you can encourage those you know to do the same. Inspire your friends and family to get involved with you. Use your influence and money for good, and good will come back to you.

Hosting community events

Contributing to the community and being a valuable source to provide help and support is something you have to be passionate about, as there is most often no financial gain. I believe the love to give selflessly is essential to making it work. It can take up a great deal of time, energy, money, and sleep.

It is often easy to find reasons not to host a community event, too much debt, more important priorities. However, a community event can create enthusiasm and excitement. It can help promote a cause that has lasting benefits for all involved. Also, a community event can lead to a rise in volunteerism, which promotes civic virtues.

In 2014, I decided to host my first major community event with the support of my girlfriends. I wanted to show my support to other women entrepreneurs, allowing them to showcase their talents and give to a charity at the same time. I decided that all proceeds would go to Canada's leading child and youth mentoring charity, Big Brothers Big Sisters, in its division closest to my area. As a team we worked to make it happen.

Not only did we bring awareness to the community about a charity they knew little about, but we also had a hand in growing the business of the 24 other self-employed females who participated. We were able to connect people of like minds for a great cause. We were able to write a check for one of the higher donations they had seen from a third-party event. I would have to say that is was a very proud moment!

Mentoring

Having a mentor to show me the way and prevent me from making some mistakes in life has helped me. We learn much from the mistakes of others, saving us hurt and time of our own. I feel strongly that once you reach a certain level of experience or success you should be able to give back and share your wealth of knowledge and experience.

Until recently, I didn't realize the amount of people that considered me a mentor. I had noticed an increase in the amount of people who would call for my opinion or advice, but not until I grew my presence through social media did I receive an increase in messages from people in other countries that referred to me as inspiring.

The influx in acknowledgement has led to the realization that as much as I find the importance in having mentors for myself, I too can give back and mentor others. I have a plethora of life experience and life lessons to share with the world. The good roads and the bad roads travelled can be used as lessons to others of what to do and what not to do.

Although I have no formal training or classroom certification as a mentor, I have the school of hard knocks under my belt. I may not be an international household name just yet, but I'm successful. I'm successful at helping others, at being a good nurturer and mother. I'm known for being an ethical, fair human being. These are not qualities you learn in a classroom, and I'm more than happy to share that with anyone else willing to learn.

A young woman about ten years younger than me had started with an e-mail to me inquiring how I managed my real estate career as a single mother. In my efforts to be transparent and real, I gave her an opening to ask life questions as they came up. I was humbled that she wanted my opinion and didn't give her that "I'm too busy for you" reply. We connected on social media and she regularly reached out for advice and inspiration. She felt comfortable sharing with me that she too had come from a place of lack and admired my qualities and heart to help others. I saw a piece of myself in her; I felt her pain when she spoke.

She confessed one day that she looked up to me and I was her mentor. I was humbled. As much as I strived to be a mentor to my children, I was touched that another woman would see me as a mentor. I am far from perfect, but I am a child of God and love the feeling of doing his work here on earth. She had me in tears one evening when I opened my social media to a notification from her. The post was a beautiful tribute to me but these words stuck out to me, "She's taken me under her wing and expects nothing in return. I think she has restored my faith in humanity!"

There will always be those less fortunate than us. We may never be able to remedy all the wrong in the world. Changing and affecting the lives of a few at a time is far greater than doing nothing at all. When you grow up having less than, it builds an appreciation when you do have. Being able to give back to others can change how they view life. If you can improve the life of another human being by giving or sharing what you have, life will reward you for your generosity. Sow your seeds and God will nourish it, and you will reap your harvest!

Chapter 14

- EMOTIONAL INTELLIGENCE, SELF-LOVE, AND SELF-IMAGE -

Emotional intelligence, also known as your EQ, is just as important if not more so than your Intellectual intelligence (IQ). Being book smart isn't enough to be successful in life. Your EQ impacts the way you interact with others and the way that you behave. Poor EQ can lead many book smart individuals down the road of failure.

Emotional intelligence gives us the ability to communicate effectively, empathize with other people, use, identify, and manage emotions in positive ways to relieve stress, overcome challenges, and defuse conflict. After dealing with my adversities, it has raised my emotional intelligence. I am now able to recognize my own emotional state and the emotional state of others. This has allowed me to engage with those around me, creating closer connections.

I've been able to use this understanding of emotions and why people act the way that they do to form healthier relationships, achieve success in work environments, and lead a full life. Instead of getting upset or building animosity towards another for them being who they are, I assess why they act in the way that they do and deal with them accordingly.

Emotional intelligence affects your work performance. It can help you deal with social difficulties in the work place, motivate and lead others, and excel in your career. In real estate, I strive to strike emotional cords with my clients to build trust. I read their body language and tone to gauge how they feel about a property. If a husband and wife disagree on parts of a property, I'm able to dissect and explain to one why the other may see things differently. When you are able to understand both sides of view, it's easier to break it down so others can also see it.

Your physical health is affected by your EQ. Our emotional/mental health affects the physical. When we are unable to manage stress it leads to health issues. It can raise blood pressure, suppress immune system, speed aging, and increase the risk of heart attack and stroke. During the beginning of my divorce I had never dealt with such high levels of stress in my life. I was in and out of the hospital. My stress caused migraines, high blood pressure, and I seemed to have a cold all the time. I had to find outlets and learn to manage my stress before it killed me.

Emotional intelligence affects your mental health, making you vulnerable to anxiety and depression. If you cannot manage your emotions and understand why you feel the way that you do, you're prone to mood swings. Lashing out was common for me during my adversities. I knew why I felt angry, but I had not learned to deal with it. I had to learn this the hard way. I hurt the feelings of people I claimed to love and when they chose to step back from me I felt lonely and isolated.

After months without them, I felt it. I didn't want to be alone so I practiced controlling my temper. I had to think before I spoke or acted. How will this possibly turn out? Do I want that outcome? It was a trial-and-error process, and managing your emotions will be different for each person as we all cope differently, but acknowledging it is a start.

Our relationships are affected by our EQ. If you can't express how you feel or understand how others feel, you can't build strong bonds. We need to be able to control our emotions to hold connections with others. If we don't have healthy relationships, it has a negative effect on how we feel about ourselves. It is detrimental to the strength of our self-love.

What is self-love, really? The definition may differ depending on who you ask. Each person may have different ways of loving themselves, and we all have different levels of appreciation of who we are. Do you love yourself? If you've answered yes, are you doing things that display that? Coming from a place of low self-esteem to a place where I love myself more than anyone else can was a process. It's a daily process to be quite honest. Something that I get better at as each day goes by.

Growing up as a tomboy I didn't care much for my appearance. I didn't feel attractive or feminine. I cared for myself enough not to do anything detrimental to my health, but I wouldn't say I loved myself. I always had a strong mind growing up and understood that I was a child of God, but my actions didn't display self-love. To be honest, I didn't really understand self-love until my early thirties.

EMOTIONAL INTELLIGENCE, SELF-LOVE, AND SELF-IMAGE

I had always been the type to put others first, leaving myself for last. From the time I became pregnant as a teenager, especially during my marriage, up until the past couple of years as a single mother, I was putting everyone else's needs before mine. I was skipping out on providing myself with the necessities of life, forgetting that if something happened to me I could not provide for them. I was queen of giving myself "what's left" from dinner after everyone else had a chance to eat, what's left of the hot water after everyone else has had a chance to shower, what's left of my time after I did what everyone else needed done, and what's left after the day is done doing for others to rest.

During my soul-searching after my sister passed away and I was trying to heal, I found doing things for myself felt good. Not just good physically and mentally but good for the soul. I was tired of crying, tired of hurting, and sick from mourning. I began to easily lose myself in anything that felt good for my soul. It left me feeling guilty to start as I was taking away from the time I could be doing things for someone else that had a need. Spending time doing things for myself seemed like a guilty pleasure. I was ashamed to tell others when I was doing what seemed like sneaking off to enjoy time relieving stress or pampering my outer shell.

I began with going to the gym, and I would spend an hour a day in there to take time for myself and focus on me. While in there, I cleared my head and zoned out of reality. I meditated on life and gave thanks for my ability to move and do the physical things we take for granted. I would be on the treadmill enjoying the lyrics to my favorite feel-good songs staring into space creating a happy place in my head. One of my favorite classes in the gym was dancing to Latin music in Zumba class, zoning out to the up-tempo beat, getting lost in the movements as I tried to keep up with the instructor. My mind was so focused on mastering the moves as I enjoyed the music blasting through the speakers that my hour would fly by.

By the end of a good Zumba class, I was sweating, panting, trying to catch my breath, and sore from working my lower body. I loved the feeling of the class and found it therapeutic. It was my time away from the kids and my responsibilities as a mother. My phone was either stored away or the ringer turned off so it was a much-welcomed break from work, social media, or anyone else that needed me.

Not only did that boost my energy but it also affected my mood over all. I was boosting my level of self-love by improving the condition of my shell, my love vessel. The changes I saw in my body had me feeling more confident in my appearance. I felt better in my clothes and was inspired to buy new clothing as a reward. Spoiling myself with new clothing made me feel good when I got dressed to go out and face the world. It was a snowball effect. I will address the effects of self-image shortly.

I slowly began to find other things to do more for myself that added variety other than the trips to the gym. I took up reading books. I had never had the attention span to complete an adult-size novel. I would lose interest in the book or lose focus from the distraction of others and not complete the entire book. I began to read at night after I put my kids to bed. The house was quiet and the rest of the world was either in bed also or winding down their day and wouldn't disturb me. When I realized how much I was enjoying reading before bed, I took up reading self-help books.

Books that inspired growth in who I was and gave tips on how to be the person I wanted to be filled the storage space on my iPad. These self-help books built on my depth of self-love and brought to light the importance of accepting who I was and being true to self. The more I read, the more I absorbed and found myself speaking about what I was reading during conversation. It inspired more soul-searching.

When I was in my state of transition of massive change in my life for the umpteenth time, I re-evaluated the people I was surrounded by. Loving myself played a large role in that. How we feel about ourselves shows through how we allow others to treat us. When my awareness of this opened up I was quick to remove myself from anyone that didn't respect my personal boundaries. I didn't care how long I knew them, if they were family, or if they felt they deserved my respect. I loved myself enough to know that their connection was not healthy.

At the time I had agreed to be a SisterTalk Circle Leader, I was going through the beginning phase of my self-love journey. SisterTalk Circles are empowerment circles where women meet monthly to have authentic conversations about life, love, relationships, and careers. Through open and honest dialogue, women tackle the obstacles that prevent them from creating the life they love and deserve.

I was certified through the program and trained and given the tools to help other women own their stories, manage shame talk, and embrace self-love. By the time I completed the course and had worked through the 13 modules, I was more sure of myself and why I had allowed things to happen in the past as well as why I had allowed others to treat me less than I deserved, even when I knew I was a child of God that deserved better.

We need the love and support of the people around us to stay motivated and on track. Having a small community to encourage the self-love journey and spread the positivity makes a world of difference. Positivity is contagious. Even if we were all at different stages in our self-love journey, we had a common denominator. Together we collectively had the desire to see the next woman succeed on this journey and we held each other accountable.

The self-love journey removed the shame from my past experiences and allowed me to be transparent. I am not my past. I no longer live there so I have nothing to be ashamed of. I've accepted my process in creating who I am today and I can say, "I love Makini Smith." I don't need anyone's approval but God's. Validation is for parking, not people. Many may not love me, but I love me and God loves me; that's all that matters.

Once removing the shame and being comfortable to do as I please, I now openly treat myself to love gifts. It could be a pair of shoes, an outfit, a trip to get my nails done, or dessert. I treat myself like I would treat any other person that I love. Special treatment and doing things to show love is something we all deserve, but if we are not showing love to ourselves then how can we expect other people to do so. How do you treat yourself? Are you in love with the person in the mirror?

There is a fine line between confidence and conceit. Being confident in who you are in a humble way and not giving the impression that you are better than anyone else is the best way to display your love for self. When you take that self-love to an extreme and have the belief of hierarchy, you come across as arrogant. That can deepen to the level of narcissism. Not everyone will understand your love for self and may even perceive it as such. It is not your job to convince anyone of anything; your actions should speak for themselves.

My self-love has evolved into my self-image and why I represent myself with pride in the way that I do. Since college, I have been known for my fashion sense or my style when I am seen in public. I was raised loving fashion, as my mother was in the industry since before I was born. Even as a tomboy in my younger years, my shoes would match my shirt or some form of coordinating was happening in my ensemble.

How we feel about ourselves comes across in our appearance. I feel that people treat you how you show them they should, so if I show up in dirty, ripped clothing, and not looking put together, that is how people will deal with you. If we base our self-worth on the outside world, we will never be capable of self-love. We must first love ourselves and let the outside world evaluate us off of that.

I dress how I want to be treated and according to where I am going. I wouldn't wear a track suit to church or a gown to watch my son play basketball. When I am relaxing and enjoying the company of friends, I know they love me and I can be in comfortable leisure wear. My tomboy comes out and I love baseball hats and sneakers, so that is usually what they will get. I don't want them to treat me differently than my other friends, so even if I'm coming from a previous engagement that required fancy clothing, I bring a change of clothes so we can enjoy each other's company without the elephant in the room of the only person dressed up.

When I have business meetings, I feel it is important to make a good first impression. I am still an introvert and can come across as shy, so my outfit makes the statement for me. I am dressed professionally but I am sure to stand out from my bright colours, fancy shoes, or statement piece accessory. Unfortunately, people judge others by appearance and I don't want to leave a bad impression based on what I looked like that day.

As God's child, I am royalty, no matter what my circumstance. I'm not saying I am better than anyone else. I am saying being a pauper is not my birthright. Feeling worthy requires you to see yourself in a brighter light. When the children of the royal family are born, they are trained to dress and act according to their stature. They are dressed in decadent clothing no matter where they are and brought up believing that it is their birthright to live a glorious life. What makes you any different?

We are love so love is within us; it is our purpose. It begins with us. We are all connected. If I can love me, then I can better love others in the process, healing them and the world. The amount of money in your bank account or your wallet doesn't define you. Society segregates class by their income. Money means nothing to God. Your worth is in your core. You and I are no different from the kings and queens of countries around the world. If we are wounded, we all bleed blood. If a fire were to strike the earth, we are all reduced to the same thing. If God is King and we are his children, then what does that mean? That is why I carry myself the way that I do and why self-image is important to me.

EMOTIONAL INTELLIGENCE, SELF-LOVE, AND SELF-IMAGE

No matter my circumstance or how much money I have, I've been consistent in my self-image to the public. Self-love isn't a one-time event; it's an endless process. I have struggled with many adversities, but no one would ever know unless I chose to share that with them. Not because I have anything to hide, but because of how I want to be treated. I don't like the feeling of being the victim. I don't need anyone feeling sorry for me. I'm certainly not looking for the pity party and have no desire to be a guest of one much less the host. My adversities have buried who I am at times, but they will not destroy me. If I truly believe that God is in control and I have faith, then why do I need to make a big deal of how bad one situation is to the rest of the world when I know that it won't last? I embrace my own affection and appreciation.

If I draw more attention to the negative, I will only attract more of it. That's not what I want so that is not what I put out. My self-image on the Internet is a reflection of that. What I post on social media is the highlights of the positive. I have just as much negative moments as the next guy, but I understand the magnetics of life. I have no desire to attract that negative energy and have it grow in my life. It is like a cancer that spreads quickly and is looking to kill and destroy whatever it gets its hands on.

I see people all the time on social media focusing on the negative situations in their lives. They complain and post about drama and it attracts more of it. The comments and consequences that follow are very rarely positive. The negative energy is picked up and repels the positive people as they begin to see these people in a negative light. It's a result of the energy that person gave off and now they have tarnished their self-image.

Due to the positive self-image that I have portrayed, it gives others the impression that my life is perfect. There is no such thing as perfect. I simply don't need a mass of uneducated opinions on my situation or circumstance. It's that simple. Opinions do not change the facts nor will the commentaries fix a situation. The reason so many continue to suffer is that they are too concerned with the opinions of those that have no idea what they are talking about.

I choose to share the positives and focus on the happy and inspiring moments because that's what I want to focus on, and that's the image I choose to portray. I choose to attract more positive into my life; I desire the company of like-minded individuals. As for the negatives, God is in control. He will take care of my struggles and give me guidance because he knows what's best. I pray to him for direction.

I was diagnosed with fibromyalgia after having my son back in 2006 after suffering from symptoms for years. Fibromyalgia is a disorder characterized by widespread muscle pain accompanied by fatigue, sleeplessness, memory, and mood issues. Researchers believe that fibromyalgia amplifies painful sensations by affecting the way your brain processes pain signals. Symptoms sometimes begin after a physical trauma, surgery, infection or significant psychological stress. In other cases, symptoms gradually accumulate over time with no single triggering event.

Women are much more likely to develop fibromyalgia than men. Many people who have fibromyalgia also have tension headaches, anxiety, and depression. I refuse to take medication as most of them have made me drowsy and unable to carry out my motherly duties. I haven't told many people that I have this, not due to shame but simply because I do not want to be treated differently. I have survived the last eight years by God's grace and have been able to accomplish more than those that are perfectly healthy. I value my image as a strong woman and would never want special treatment or be viewed as having a disability because I am an able body that defies limits on a daily basis.

While there is no cure for fibromyalgia, a variety of medications can help control symptoms. I have always had a high pain tolerance, so I can handle most days without the help of painkillers. Due to the fact that fibromyalgia isn't something you can visibly see, no one would ever tell by looking at me and most people I have told often forget. I don't run around using it as a crutch or constantly complain about the symptoms. I focus on my ability to do what I am blessed to do. I know myself well enough to know what I can tolerate and try not to push myself over the edge.

What does this have to do with self-image and self-love? Everything. If I can love myself despite what I have to deal with every day, so can you. If I can control the image of myself that I portray to others, then so can you.

Here are a few tips to improving your EQ, self-love, and self-image:

Start your day right

Begin with prayer/meditation and focus on being a better person. Embrace yourself in light. Inhale and exhale love. Follow that with a few minutes of journaling or reading of the word for reflection. I begin with a 365-day devotional book by Joyce Meyer called Starting Your Day Right that helps me begin each day focused on God's will for my life.

Affirmations

Repetition is the key to improving on anything. Use affirmations daily to train your mind to become more positive. I've mentioned this before and I will say it again, if you tell yourself a lie often enough you will start to believe it. I keep some next to my sink and read them as I brush my teeth. I keep some on the wall in my office. My favourite of all is "I'm rich in relationships and love."

Be grateful and enjoy life

Appreciate that you woke up this morning as many did not get that chance. Appreciate your gifts, beauty, and intelligence. Try something new today. Go somewhere you've never been, order something different off of the menu, do something you've never done before. Make the effort to expand your knowledge on something as small as the flavour of a fruit to something larger like learn a new language. I'm always open to trying new and exciting things. Even if I didn't enjoy it, I at least got to experience it.

Own your infinite potential

There are limitless opportunities available to you if you love yourself enough to be open to them. Let go of fear and live in faith. Remove urgency and haste, just relax, and know that everything happens in its own timing and not when we want them to. Trust in your abilities, do good to others, and the universe will reward you.

Engage in personal and spiritual development

Faith is the foundation for EQ, self-love, and self-image. No matter what your religious belief, believing in something opens your heart and soul. Exploring spirituality opens your mind to new thoughts, feelings, and emotions that help us to understand ourselves and others. Be coachable. Forever be a student and don't assume you know everything. Life really is a journey that we learn from as we grow. Be open to love and learn on a deeper level. Even one step at a time is a step in the right direction. Learn from your mistakes and move forward. It's all a part of the growth process. Every experience I've had has been a part of my learning and healing process.

Do what's best for you

Everything we need is inside of us. God provides us the tools to figure out the problems. Your intuition is the sign many don't pay enough attention to. In television they use the visual of the angel on one shoulder giving you advice and the devil on the opposite side trying to do the same. The angel is your higher self telling you what's best and the louder voice of the devil is your ego filling you with doubt. Choose the higher route.

Make time for fun.

Self-love requires play, relaxation, and enjoyable interactions. All work and no play is a sad way to spend your day. Love yourself enough to do the things that make you and others happy. Laughter is good for the soul and so is peace and quiet. I take time to laugh every day. Especially if I'm in a bad mood, I have friends I can call who are sure to give me a good laugh, and when they are not available there are plenty of things on the Internet that make me laugh out loud.

Get professional help. There will be times when we get stuck. Lord knows I have. We deserve happiness, love, and acceptance. Get the assistance of a doctor, counselor, support group, or coach. Don't ever feel ashamed to ask for help with your mental health. We have no issues running to the doctor for our physical health, so what's the difference.

Chapter 15

- DADDY'S LITTLE GIRL -

"Honor thy father and mother (which is the first commandment with promise)" (Ephesians 6:2).

I have made much reference to my mother, the strong woman that raised me full time, but I will always be my daddy's little girl. I have an unconditional, unprecedented, undying love for the man that helped create me. He wasn't able to raise me full-time, but I am part of his DNA and I have inherited all of him that God chose to give me. Studies dealing with long-term consequences of parents' divorce during childhood show that it usually weakens the emotional bond between parent and child later on in life. This is even more so with non-resident fathers.

My parents split when I was a year old and eventually divorced. I have no memory of ever living with my father, but my mother was mature enough to never paint a bad picture of him to me. I don't ever recall hearing my mother bash my father as a person. She struggled to provide and make ends meet on her own but never referenced my father's absence or financial contribution. My father has not lived in the same country as me for the majority of my life, but that hasn't had any effect on my love and appreciation for him.

I remember growing up and at times only seeing my father once or twice in a year. Cell phones were not around and it must have been very expensive for long-distance calls, so some visits were unexpected but a pleasant surprise. I would be in the neighbourhood playing with friends and see him pull in or spot him walking up to our front door. I would sprint to him and wrap my arms around him like I hadn't seen him in years. He would hug me so tight that I would melt like ice cream on a hot summer's day.

Our visits were never long, so I would cherish every second. He would take me for a drive and allowed me to bring one friend. It would be a drive to the store for candy and treats or to Dairy Queen or some other place that served desserts. Till this day I have an obsession with the Peanut Buster Parfait from Dairy Queen and going out for dessert to put me in a happy place. Going out for dessert brings me back to the excitement and special moments with daddy.

I recall a trip to the original Wimpy's Diner in Scarborough, Ontario. It took me forever to decide on what dessert I wanted until I finally agreed to try the pecan pie. I barely touched it. I didn't care for the pie; I just cared about the quality time with my father. I remember that clear as day but probably couldn't tell you the events of my day yesterday. The memories of the little time I spent bonding with my father are all positive and embedded into the movie I play in my head.

In the study I read about the effects of divorce on children, the general view was that children benefit from continued relationships with their fathers except when the father has been abusive or incompetent. Yet I continue to see women holding resentment toward men because they grew up without their father in the home. They have this anger that their father moved on to another woman and didn't try to make things work for the family. They see them as a deadbeat dad. They then build this animosity and let everything the father does get under their skin and it becomes a snowball effect to all men in their lives as they grow older.

In my opinion, what happened between my parents has nothing to do with me. My father loves me. End of story. I could play the blame game and be angry at my father for not being around more when I was younger, but what would that solve? He didn't even live in the same country. He preferred to live in the islands with his new family where he was born. All of that negative emotion put in motion to cause everyone unnecessary stress when I can use the same energy or less to be grateful for the moments I did receive.

My father had 18 children. During his marriage to my mother, she bore three for him: my sister that passed away, my elder brother, and me. It's not my place to pass judgment on his choices to have multiple other children. As his child, I am grateful that he still makes me feel special regardless of the number of children he has. From a young age, I was able to understand that my father had other children and responsibilities. The moments we shared I cherished because they made me feel special. There are a large percentage of men with multiple children who do not take care of their responsibilities. I have to acknowledge his efforts because when he was with me, it was about me.

He would fly me to the islands for holidays to stay with him and his new family that included four new siblings, and I would have the week filled with special activities. Learning to swim in the ocean, horseback riding, picking tropical fruit, and sightseeing made up much of my visits. My father is filled with knowledge and loves to share. Most trips we would visit historic sites, and he would explain the history behind them. His housekeeper would have breakfast ready when I woke up in the morning and fix me lunch when I was ready.

When I first arrived, daddy would pull out the red carpet and give me the royal treatment. He would take my younger sister (half-sister) and I to the grocery store to pick out all of my favourite foods. I would walk up and down the aisles selecting my favorite cereal, juice, snacks, and everything else my heart desired. He wanted me to be as comfortable as possible for my stay for the week. I had my own room that had a waterbed with my own en-suite washroom for my stay that I would ask my sister to join me in so I wasn't alone.

My father's home consisted of him, his new wife, my three brothers, and one sister. It always seemed as though everyone was excited to see me when I arrived. The hugs, kisses, and affection felt genuine. I was never treated negatively and always enjoyed my stay. I know my situation was not a conventional one, and I was very fortunate. Acknowledging that is exactly where my gratitude comes from. Everyone's perception is based on their experience. Even if it was a few times a year that I was able to have overnights with my father, he made them count.

Some would call that nothing to be excited about; I call it gratitude. Some could argue that that handful of moments every year doesn't make him a great father; I say it's better than many. I could count on a birthday phone call if he wasn't in the country. He may not have been physically present regularly with all of his children, but he did his best to put in the effort. I knew that he could be counted on if I needed anything. I have siblings that were privileged enough to have daddy pay their school fees for private school. I know he did his best for all of his children when he could, and knowing how many of us exist makes me appreciate his efforts.

The real deadbeats are the women that keep the children away from loving fathers for selfish reasons. If a father is involved and wants to participate, that should be appreciated. His efforts should be acknowledged and he should play a role in the child's life as long as he isn't harming the child in any way. There are many factors that could come into play as to why a woman would not want her child's father involved, but the most important factor is, how this will affect the child.

Today, it is too common to hear stories about fathers that show no effort in the lives they helped create and bring into this world. It's sad and heartbreaking both as a child raised by a single mother and as a woman that is a single mother. These little people did not ask to be here and it's selfish of any person that is involved in their creation to not participate. Where would we be if God turned his back on us?

The man was created to MANage; he was meant to be a MANager. His role is MANagement. He is made to take care of what he creates. My father has succeeded in his ability to take responsibility of his children and has had a significant influence in my life now as an adult. My father was a provider. He provided for me financially when he could, he provided memories I will never forget, and most importantly he provided a standard of how I wanted to be treated by a man.

He was my first experience with being treated special by a man. He has displayed time and time again that chivalry isn't dead when he opens car doors for me. He takes off my shoes when I am unable to. From the time I was a little girl he has taken me on dates. He has taught me that a man should make me feel as though nothing else matters when we are spending quality time together. All of these things I learned from my relationship with my father. "But now abideth faith, hope, love, these three; and the greatest of these is love" (1 Corinthians 13:13).

As a grown woman now, I can look back on the relationship of my parents over the last thirty-something years and say that he also did an amazing job at showing me how a woman should be treated by his interaction with my mother. Neither parent is perfect, but they have remained friends over the years. My father still visits my mother when he is in town and cares for her well-being. There is a love there that may never die. There is nothing more pleasant to God than the unity of his people.

It's a great feeling to be able to host a family function and have both parents in the same room making jokes and having a good time. To see the unity of my family that stems from the two people I love the most, which encourages the bonds of siblings that have not been created jointly, and feel the love is priceless. It's a blessing to experience. "Behold, how good and how pleasant it is for brethren to dwell together in unity!" (Psalm 133:1).

I have a very large family thanks to my father. We don't have a conventional family, but the bond is there. Of the large amount of siblings I have, only two were conceived by my mother and father. Not once have I ever looked at any of the others as my half-brother or half-sister. This was established by my father from the beginning. "This is your brother or sister," was how we were introduced.

The title was set and given the respect for our parents; it stuck. Forming bonds with my siblings was something my father encouraged from the beginning also. He would make the phone call so we could talk on the phone or make the trips to pick children up so we could have time together as siblings. My trips to the islands for holidays gave plenty of time to associate with my siblings while daddy had to leave for work early in the day.

At the present time, the majority of my siblings reside in Canada, and as adults my father has stepped back and allowed us to make our own judgment call. The habits of unity have not left me. I make the effort to stay connected to my siblings and keep up with how they and their families are doing. Family and relationships are important to me now because it was taught growing up. The effects left on children, whether their parents are together or divorced, have an impact on the type of people they grow up to be as adults.

My brothers have become my protectors, and I love them dearly. My love for them is so much so that each one of my children has a strong resemblance to one of my brothers. These boys, like my father, treat me like I'm a queen. They check on me regularly and do what they can to help. They continue to play a huge role in my life. Knowing how hard I love, they check my blind spots in my relationships with potential male partners and female friends. They cover me.

The way that my brothers and my father treat me has been admired by many. One summer my brother wanted to treat his daughter to a weekend at an indoor water park in Niagara Falls, Ontario. He invited his closest friends to bring their family and join our family members with our children. I had invited my friend to come along with her two children.

She stayed in the family suite with my family and was in awe at how well the men in my family took care of me. She was extremely surprised at how attentive they were with the children and how much pride they looked after them. It was like a weekend with male nannies to her. She felt comfortable releasing her own two children into the care of my father and brothers.

The men made sure the children ate, played fair, had enough blankets, and sat around telling jokes with them at the end of the night. She herself was very much a daddy's girl but was extremely surprised with the level of love and endearment that was displayed between us that weekend. She was most shocked at my father's level of energy to run around and play with the children. He was like a grown child once they got him going.

When we returned home, she expressed the level of respect she now had for the men in my family. My father had loaded her and her children's luggage into her vehicle, made sure seatbelts and car seats were buckled up, and hugged them all good-bye. Her exact words were, "Their own father doesn't even do that!" I was proud that my father had set a new standard for her. She too had assumed the man with many children didn't participate in their lives. She was able to see firsthand the active role he plays in the lives of his children and his grandchildren.

I will forever be my daddy's little girl.

DADDY'S LITTLE GIRL

Chapter 16

- LOVE AND RELATIONSHIPS -

I'm addicted to love. I get high on it. It's the crash afterwards when things don't work out that scares me a little. Am I not afraid to love after being betrayed? Am I not afraid to be vulnerable and take that risk? How do I trust another man?

What happened in the past is gone. It didn't kill me. I'm still alive. My heart still beats. Yes, I got hurt, but why should that stop me from participating in relationships. When a child gets hurt playing in the playground, do we expect them to never play again? NO!

So why is the first thing we are expected to do as humans is hang up our dating hat and be sour forever and ever, amen? Conquering that fear of being vulnerable, letting someone close enough to hurt me, and trusting again has been a process.

One of our basic human needs is love/connection. Depending on whose study you follow, we have 5-7 basic human needs. No matter which one you want to believe, love is in all of them. God created us to be full of love.

Although each person is unique, every one of us is built with a nervous system that functions the same way. Love is a fundamental need that we have in common and our behaviour is an attempt to meet those needs. Our nervous systems are encoded to meet those needs. The means in which we do so is unlimited. For myself, I feel like strong-hearted people seek out to fill this need almost as much as food and water.

"A relationship isn't for the selfish, the weak-hearted, or those who are easily deterred. True lovers don't give up until they find exactly what they're looking for" — Rob Hill Sr. (The Heart Healer).

I have to say that this quote describes me in every sense. I am selfless, strong hearted, steadfast, and I won't give up until I get my happy ending!

When God created mankind, he created Adam and Eve. Eve is created from one of Adam's ribs to be Adam's companion. We were not created to be alone. Woman balances man. Man balances woman. "It is not good for the man to be alone. I will make a helper suitable for him."(Genesis 2:18).

The year after my divorce was finalized, I met a man that, at the time, I felt was made just for me. I felt he was almost too good to be true. You know the type that says the things from his mouth those authors like Derrick Jaxn posts about on his social media?

"If catering to your woman is lame, then I want to be the most picnic planning, foot massaging, toe sucking, breakfast cooking, forehead kissing, love letter writing, back rubbing, date night cuddling, flower bringing, daily praying, and marriage proposing lame alive" or "You've been working so hard, keeping yourself from crying, and checking on everyone else to make sure they're good. Now relax, and let me appreciate you for being you" Derrick Jaxn (The Self Love Ambassador).

The stuff that just sounds like good poetry but is hard to find in real life came in the form of a text, email, or on a card delivered with flowers. He had me from the start, but I was too scared to let him know. I wasn't about to hand over my heart. I hadn't fully healed yet.

It all began in Norfolk, Virginia with my girlfriend and I trying to escape our busy realtor lives for a few days. We had decided on the getaway the week before New Year's. Things had become hectic for us, and she had a friend out there that owned a local bar/club. He invited us out to ring in the New Year and I didn't care at the time where I went, I just needed a break from reality.

We arrived in Virginia the night before the big party at his club. The night of New Year's, I didn't care if I went to a party or stayed at home watching Netflix with my best friend. We had binge-watched reality television all day. Neither of us watched much television back home since we were both extremely busy realtors in Toronto at the time. We had to force ourselves to get ready. I believe we rolled in 30-45 minutes before midnight.

As we entered the party, we were escorted to the booth that was reserved for us. On our walk towards VIP, I noticed a man at the bar inhaling some chicken wings. He was kind of cute but was clearly having his fill before indulging in drinks for the celebration. He caught my attention as we made our way up the stairs but nothing spectacular.

I was never really much of a dancer at parties, more the people watcher type as I rock back and forth to the music. I felt out of place in this unfamiliar city and was up in VIP, higher than the crowd for everyone to see. It felt as if the spotlights were on me, front and centre stage. I was a little tense and it must have been evident. I wanted God to open up the floor and just swallow me whole and spit me back out some place where I could be out of sight.

As I sat on the arm of the couch, I felt eyes on me. My girl handed me a drink and said, *"Relax."*

I could never handle much alcohol and didn't like the feeling of being not 100 percent in control of my body, so usually I would nurse one drink all night and offer to be the designated driver. That was not going to be the case tonight. I took a sip and thought how uptight I must look sitting on the arm of this chair in VIP just staring into the crowd. I was there to have fun. I wanted to have fun. I just couldn't relax. I gulped my drink and asked for another. My girl handed me a shot of cognac and a separate glass with my next drink. I got up to take the shot with her as we made a toast to the New Year and our growing sisterhood.

The liquid courage began to sink in and I was rocking back and forth to the music. I had finally begun to relax. I didn't even see her leave my side. I looked up to see my girl coming towards me with the guy that was inhaling the chicken wings at the bar earlier. His face lit up with a beautiful smile as we made eye contact. I couldn't help but smile back. He was much better looking up close than when he was leaning over the bar being a human vacuum cleaner.

There was instant chemistry. He had a charismatic way about him. I wasn't very good at small talk, but he kept my attention. I rocked back and forth to the music as he chatted me up. Before I knew it, the ten-second count down was going and we were smiling and staring each other in the eyes. I felt like Cinderella and he was Prince Charming. I didn't want it to end at midnight.

The crowd screamed "HAPPY NEW YEAR!" and he kissed me on the forehead and we embraced with a tight hug. The clock had struck midnight. I don't recall what heels I had on that night, but I didn't lose my glass slipper. The rest of the night seemed unreal. We talked, we laughed, and we danced until the lights came on. Neither he nor I wanted the night to end. We hung around as the people cleared out. Family members and staff of the owner began cleaning. My girlfriend looked at me and smiled. "Don't you look happy? You should take a picture and see how cute you two look together."

I handed her my phone and she took our picture. In it, we both had a look in our eyes as if we knew it was the start of something great. They say a picture is worth a thousand words. That picture captured our instant connection. It was as if we were already a couple. The connection was not just physical. I felt like I knew his spirit. The energy was pure.

That night was the start of one of my most memorable relationships. It was the start of my first long distance relationship, and it was the relationship that set the bar for how I wanted to be treated by any other man that would come along after. He set a precedent and I know they say it is not wise to compare, but any man that made an attempt to court me had to come close to the way he treated me and made me feel.

He had just upped my standards when it came to how I should be treated by a man. I felt so new. I didn't know what I was missing before this point. He had me curious if most American men were the same. I know better, but I had never heard of a man in my city that literally spoke poetry and wanted a happily ever after the way I did.

The long distance forced us to get to know one another on a deeper level. We had to get creative in doing acts of service to show we cared. It was six months of all the things you see in romance movies. Having things delivered to my house and vice versa, sweet poetic words via email, text message conversations that never ended, and phone calls every night. His friends referred to me as "Toronto" and my friends called him "Mr. Virginia."

I had no idea I could love so hard again after what I had been through. I had tried dating but my guard was always up. I was always waiting for the other shoe to fall. I felt I could be vulnerable with him. He just came across so genuine. No hidden agenda. With the distance between us, the attraction had to be far more than just physical. I felt a strong spiritual connection. Like God himself sent this man to restore all the hope that had been lost.

He cared about everything that was important to me. He would remember things I had told him about my kids and we would talk about them like they were ours. Mr. Virginia hadn't even met my children but made me feel that he was up for the challenge. He was a God fearing man that loved just as hard as I did. He knew how to show he was paying attention in all the right ways.

His first visit to Toronto was one I will not soon forget. From our dates out on the town to us grocery shopping together so he could cook me dinner in my own kitchen. He was the perfect gentleman. He said grace before our meals, held doors, and massaged my hands as we talked. Through his words and actions he was everything I thought was only what you read about in romance novels.

My next trip to Virginia was filled with fun dates and sightseeing. We had restaurant dinner dates, went go karting, wine tasting, and more. He made sure I had an amazing time and wanted to return. It was so hard to leave. Both our eyes watered as we kissed good-bye at the airport.

As the months passed, we had talks about how to close the distance. The conversation of him spending the warmer months in Toronto or the possibility of me packing up the kids and moving to the USA happened a few times.

After 6 months, my high came to an end. I had made it clear that I couldn't move my kids away from their fathers. He had decided that the cold winter months in Toronto weren't for him or being so far from his family. It was a large sacrifice for both of us to make and the timing wasn't right for either of us to take a major step in that direction.

I was planning my next trip to Virginia when he kept delaying asking his boss for the Friday off of work. I had planned to arrive the Friday morning and he would pick me up from the airport. For almost 2 weeks he stalled, and I could feel it. His pattern changed. I knew something was wrong but I wasn't ready for what came next.

He messaged less, was too busy for calls, and finally said at the last hour that he couldn't get any time off approved. I had been on cloud nine for months and the uneasiness I felt was getting to me. I became distracted as my thoughts wondered to what could be the cause for the change in patterns. I didn't want to assume he had found someone else, but it didn't take rocket science to realize I was no longer a priority.

Sitting in the kitchen of my girlfriend's home, I sat and stared at my phone. She was the one that brought him to me that New Year's Eve in Virginia and seemed just as happy for me. She asked how we were doing and the look of doom came over my face. I informed her of the changes in pattern. "Just call him and ask him what's going on!" she barked.

I instantly sent a text and hit send before I could change my mind. His response sent tears down my cheek that I let roll until they dripped off the bottom of my chin. The text hurt as if he was standing in front of me telling me that we were over "I don't see the point in us continuing to fall deeper for one another and get further involved if neither of us in willing to move."

I had never been broken up with before. Every other relationship I was involved in, I was the one that ended it. That text led to a conversation of "I need a woman that can physically be here. I think we should be friends." It hurt like hell!

We never had a fight. We never had a disagreement. He just gave up on the distance. If I didn't have children, I would have packed my bags and been on the next flight to Virginia for good. I was letting the man I thought to be the love of my life walk away because I didn't want to distance my children from their biological fathers. I had a responsibility to my children, which he had full respect for. I made a sacrifice at the time to do what was best for them.

Now I know you are probably thinking 6 months is not a long time. How could I have possibly determined him the love of my life in such a short time? God does not work on our time! The spirit man does things before the flesh. The connection and familiarity we feel with someone happens before we connect with them in the flesh. I felt connected to him, and he said he felt the same.

When we meet someone we connect with on a soul level, things form much quicker than the average relationship. The familiar feeling of their spirit causes us to let our guard down. It feels as though we knew them from a past life. The intense flow of emotions can be overwhelming. It can be draining mentally, emotionally, and spiritually when the romantic idea of it is broken.

There is a higher purpose for such encounters. They force us to grow. To grow mentally, emotionally, and spiritually for "the one" we are supposed to be with. It took me a few years to realize that he wasn't meant to be Mr. Right. He was an amazing Mr. Right Now though.

I learned valuable lessons from our connection, and that is why we remain friends till this day. There is a strong connection and a feeling that we have unfinished business. We still remind each other how much we helped each other grow. He taught me how I wanted to be treated. I already knew how I didn't want to be treated as a result of my past relationships, but he made it clear exactly what I wanted in the affirmative. My father and brothers treated me like a queen and he stepped it up a notch. He raised the bar for any man that came after.

I have to admit that the crash of emotions from being on such a high hurt when I hit the floor. I put walls up around my heart higher than I had before, but I realized I was only hurting myself. I wanted to be loved, but I wouldn't let anyone else love me. I became bitter before I got better. The long distance relationship came to an end when it required a sacrifice. It would have been a large sacrifice for one of us to make, but I guess the love wasn't deep enough to do so. You can tell the difference between lust and love once it requires a sacrifice. I'm not saying he didn't love me, but he chose an out at the first sign of an obstacle rather than discuss a solution.

It was easy to spot the men I dated that just lusted after me when I heard things like "Why do you have to live so far? If you didn't live so far I could pick you up and take you out on more dates." Meanwhile they only lived 30-45 minutes away from me! My guard was up and they were out the door before they knew what was happening. NEXT! My time here on earth is too precious to waste on those that do not value me.

Guard your heart. There is nothing wrong with guarding and protecting something so gentle and fragile. The problem is when we over protect it and bury it so deep into a hole we can't get it out. If that's you, it's time to start digging. Some have buried their heart so deep they don't even know where to begin searching.

Not only have they covered up their heart far out of reach, they've built a thick layer of steel. You don't want a wall so high no one can climb over. You also don't want the extreme opposite.

Having a wall so low that you let everyone in runs your heart a great danger. Instead, build a door. That allows you to control whom you let in.

It is perfectly OK to be vulnerable. It allows your heart to feel true pleasure. You just have to know who to be vulnerable with. Take your time getting to know people and you will eventually see whom you can be vulnerable with. Time reveals all, especially if it's love.

Have you ever jumped into a relationship, gave someone your heart, only to find a few months down the road that they were not deserving? Had you taken the time to get to know them on a deeper level before handing them your heart, you would have had time to realize you were falling for someone that wasn't planning to catch you. I don't want to fall in love again; I want to stand in it. I want to be vulnerable with someone that wants to be vulnerable with me and I'm willing to keep trying until I get it right.

Fast forward to today, I have had a brutal run of cutting men off after 90 days because they simply couldn't measure up. It may seem unfair to them but I refuse to be treated any less than I deserve. I've given them three months to show me who they are and if we are compatible to build a future. As I get older, the applicants have been less as my standards become clear. I lay out who I am at the front door and if they have any issues with that then I walk away gracefully in my heels. I don't expect any man to be what I am not. I don't hold unrealistic expectations. I don't need the perfect mate; I just want my purpose mate. As a result, being single and working on my own personal growth has been the outcome. I was beginning to think that my standards were too high, and I would be single forever.

Men that appreciate a woman with standards no longer seem to be the norm, but it does exist. Every now and again God sends a representative to show that all is well in the world. The universe operates by law and order. God is very meticulous. If you ever have a desire you want fulfilled, trust me when I tell you that dreams can become reality. Prayer, affirmation, and focus can attract more than you can even ask or think. Our lives are a reflection of our thoughts and actions.

I held my ground with my standards. Literally dug my heels into the ground and refused to budge until God sent me someone that would value the jewels he has decorated my royal crown with. When I least expected it, God placed a man in my life that restored my faith in men yet again. A man that keeps finding ways to add jewels to my crown instead of trying to remove them in hopes that others will find it less appealing.

God sent a man that not only matched the amazing qualities of Mr. Virginia but gave him a run for his money. I could write an entire romance novel on the ways he showed me love through action. It was as though God took note of every request I had made for my future husband, whispered it into this mans ear and put him through training to make sure he was ready for me.

We spoke the same love language, both writers, and we shared the same views on so many things that it seemed like I was in a dream. God sent a man that appeared equally yoked. I had once watched a video of a sermon by Touré Roberts, the pastor of a church in Los Angeles, who gave the five keys to identifying your soulmate/purpose mate. Here is what I took from that:

We attract what we are. That's how the universe works. If we expect to attract the mate that complements us best, we have to stop searching and picking for ourselves as we will choose wrong. When we are ready to receive our soul mate, God will present them to us but we have to be able to identify them. Once you are able to recognize this person, they will complement your life and ensure fullness of your potential. They are more of a purpose mate as your connection will lead to love.

1. CHEMISTRY: It won't only be about looks but the spirit. The chemistry you feel will be because you are on the same frequency. The vibe will be almost perfect and you will be smitten by their spirit. Things will feel almost effortless. They will take the time to learn about you and what is important to you and vice versa: things like what calms you down when you are upset, what makes you tick, and how you like your meals prepared. But the desire will happen naturally. You will miss them the minute they are gone.

2. CONNECTION: It will feel as though you have known each other for some time. Their spirit will know you all too well. You will have a mutual/equal need to be together and want to go further with the person. Discuss future plans and goals with this person. Do you both want children? Do you both want to get married? There is a difference between love and lust. This will differentiate if the connection will be long term or short lived.

3. WHOLENESS: This will qualify the connection. You should feel whole and not co-dependent. You should be able to have your independence without them feeling insecure or

threatened. This mate doesn't drain you or fill a void, rather you complement each other. Neither person should feel that the other completes them. Both parties feel a mutual happiness for the other's accomplishments and accreditations. At any point that your faith is weary, your partner is there to help restore it.

4. DIVINE CONFIRMATION: In the spiritual world there is no such thing as coincidence. You will receive confirmation that the union was meant to be. You've prayed or meditated and God has confirmed your feelings. You've received a sign from a higher power that this person is meant for you.

5. SENSE OF PURPOSE: Before you can even attract your soul mate, you must know your purpose. They will add to that. They are a part of your purpose and you a part of theirs. You are a support system for each other. At some point you may or may not have a common purpose but you individually know what your purpose is in this life here on earth.

There is no definite way to find your soul mate, but these 5 keys may help you to identify that person should the opportunity arrive. Be patient, don't settle, and understand that God's timing may not be the same as ours.

I felt like I met my purpose mate in 2015. I almost missed the opportunity because I wasn't seeing him in that light at first. We originally connected on social media, and he didn't peak my interest. After spending time with him for work related purposes, we clicked immediately. I allowed God to take the wheel there. He's the captain of every ship I board. I let him lead my relationships, friendships, and even partnerships at this point in my life.

Time passed and we developed intense feeling for one another. This time I was ready to make the sacrifice of moving from Toronto to America for love. We grew closer, fell deeper, and both wanted to close the distance. He and I were living in our own fairytale adult world. This one hasn't ended with the happily ever after just yet, but I'm optimistic. Timing has placed the situation on hold but I'm praying that God will reset the clock when the time is right.

Whether God is saving us single people for someone special or building us so we can be prepared to receive our soul mate once they arrive, we have to keep hope alive. We can't quit now because we tried and it didn't work. How can we say that God is love and then give up on love? Isn't that giving up on God?

Chapter 17

- LIFE IS ABOUT THE JOURNEY -

Life is full of ups and down. There is no such thing as the path straight to success or the good life. We all have a different road we must travel to get where we are supposed to be. What is destined for you may not be the destiny of the next person. Enjoy the journey you have been given. Spend a little time taking in the sights and reflect on what it is that you are supposed to learn.

With life's peaks and valleys, the hustle of getting through each day, it's easy to forget to slow down and enjoy the moment. We are so busy living our own lives that we forget to make time for the people and things that bring us joy. We get so caught up in the destination that we forget to enjoy the actual journey.

For every step of the journey there is a lesson to learn. It is the trip of a lifetime and that route may not be available to take again. Those visuals may not be the same on the next ride, so take it all in. Don't be in such a rush to get to the destination that you miss out on all of life's beauty right in front of you. As the saying goes, "Stop and smell the roses." Don't be in such haste that you run right past what was boldly left there for you to see.

This life you have been given was for a purpose. Have you figured out what that purpose is? Do you know why God placed you on this earth, gave you that face, or that body? We all have a purpose here on earth and it isn't to suffer and be miserable. Appreciate all things and you will truly find happiness. Stop where you are at this moment. Really stop and be still. Listen. What do you hear? What do you see?

First you must give thanks that you have the ability to hear, as not every human being was blessed with that ability. Secondly, I want you to be appreciative that you can see your surroundings. These simple things are taken for granted by every single one of us. When was the last time you thanked God for your vision and hearing? We are like spoiled ungrateful entitled teens living in first world countries with problems for which many would give their last dollar.

When you look around you at the luxury that is your surroundings, count every single item that you should be grateful for. Now slowly begin to imagine your life if you could not have these things. That television you stare at for hours on end, what if it never existed? What would you entertain yourself with? That soft carpet beneath your feet, what if a dirt floor was all you had? Or if you are reading this on public transit, what would you do if you had to walk that route each day instead?

Do you see how much of life we take for granted and complain about? Enjoying this life is really about having gratitude for the simple things. Rushing to get rich before having understanding and the belief necessary is like being on the freight train to misery. Using the money we earn to make ourselves more comfortable and to also share it and make the lives of others more comfortable is the only way to enjoy financial wealth. Your attitude about life will determine what you get out of it. I cannot stress enough: be grateful, be grateful, and be grateful.

If you look outdoors, what in nature can you admire about the beauty of it or even the symbolism. There is much to take in and learn from something as simple as a tree. It stands tall and still but grows at a pace not visible to the human eye. Its roots planted firm as its foundation. As the seasons change, the tree prepares for what is to come. It isn't caught off guard by winter with fresh green leaves lingering. It knows the pattern of what is next and the leaves change colour and fall off. When spring comes it is alive again. The buds magically appear and the green leaves return. It's a predictable pattern.

I've slowed down and taken the time to realize that once we stop rushing through life, the lessons and predictable patterns are right there in front of us to see. Nature is a symbolism for our life. I am that tree. My roots/faith planted firm is my foundation. I go through seasons in my life. I have seasons when I know things are going to change and I have to let go of things/people before that new season comes. I can't be caught off guard with the same old habits/people lingering. When my season of hibernation and preparation has passed, I blossom once again. My life mimics the pattern of the tree.

This pattern of seasons at times feels like a struggle to me. One step forward, two steps back is more the pace of my life pattern, but I now understand that it is a part of the journey. Understanding that it is a part of what happens in life has helped me get over the hurdles much quicker. Knowing that when I come out of the valley there will be a peak is my reminder when things get hard. My life has a pattern. It is just a season.

Just as nature has the cycle of seasons that follow a predictable pattern and I can be certain that after fall comes winter and not fall again, after my down times my season will change. It is guaranteed to be a new season and not the same one on repeat. As much as my pattern has been one step forward, two steps back, I am almost certain that it is due to a lesson I did not learn the first time it was presented to me. I was probably not taking the time needed and sped past the lesson. Don't be too busy that you get consumed. " It is of Jehovah's lovingkindnesses that we are not consumed, because his compassions fail not" (Lamentations 3:22).

Thinking back, there are moments where I may have done things differently had I taken the time. I may not have learned the lesson I was supposed to learn but I did learn a lesson none the less. There are some things I may have relived the exact same way given the choice. How many times have you heard someone say, "I wish I was 20 again. The things I would have done different had I known what I know now"? There are a lot of people that didn't live life the way they had wished. Would you have done differently if you had the chance? Did you miss out on many moments in your past because you were not grateful?

Many people live in regret because they didn't freely live their lives; they were too busy following the masses. Too many people are living in remorse for not doing things the way they wanted to do them. The older I get, the more I realize that we just need to live. Be the best you that you possibly can. Stay authentic to who you are and don't get caught up trying to be who everyone else wants you to be or expects you to be. This is your life; others have their own lives to control.

Trying to go through life abiding by rules set by someone else will never bring you joy. That's a setup for stress and unhappiness. Happiness is feeling good about yourself without the need of approval from others. Some rules are meant to be broken; I prefer to make them up as I go along. If you are not hurting anyone and your heart is in the right place, then don't conform or ever apologize for being who you are. You don't require approval to live. My happiness comes from my relationship with God. I talk to him and listen for his answers. His approval is all I need.

I have been labeled all kinds of things from crazy, misfit, different, and abnormal. Whatever they label you, the fact remains, you are not meant to be the same as them. I choose to go against the grain and take the road less traveled. Make your own path. It feeds my creativity. I wasn't put on this earth to be average. I am here to be awesome in every way I can imagine.

I humbly accept the challenge of being whom and what I want to be. I accept that failure will happen, but that simply means I am one step closer to reaching my goals. I dive in head first. If I bump my head because the water was shallow, then it is a lesson learned. If I put the tip of my toe in the water, I may never get in because it feels too cold. Jump in; you will adjust to the environment. Every test we experience can make you better or bitter; the choice is yours. That problem you are facing can be a situation to make you or break you, depending on your reaction to it. I always choose to be victorious rather than the victim.

Part of the reason why we all experience such a diverse journey is because we have choices. I choose to find the positive. I choose to push past the bad times. What choices are you making that are hindering you from living your best life? What have you been telling yourself about your future? We all have a choice. If you fall, get back up and try again. It's only failure if you stay where you have fallen. Train your mind to see the positive in every situation. It begins with mindset.

Put positivity out and you will receive it in return. If someone doesn't appreciate it or a door is closed, understand that it just wasn't meant to be. Don't hold grudges or be angry. One day down the road God will show you why he closed that door when he opens other ones for you, and you can thank him. Stop letting every disappointment consume your happiness. Live! Tomorrow may not come. Nothing is ever a guarantee, so enjoy it while you can.

Dream big! What does your future hold? Start by asking yourself what is it that you want and not what your current situation will allow you to have. I get a good chuckle when people say, "You should live within your means." If you want to succeed and live a fulfilling life, then it requires you to be a little irrational at times. I think big, so I receive big. I know what I want. I have no idea how I'm going to get there, but that mindset has gotten me pretty far to start. I also expect to receive it. There is no point in saying we want something, put it up to God in prayer, have it floating in the universe but not expect it to happen.

Have high expectations out of life. If you are struggling at this very moment and you don't feel that it will end, it won't. That simple. Expect that things will improve. Have the expectation that things will turn around and God will do what he promised. Then be prepared to receive. Laugh in the face of adversity because you have the expectation that you will overcome it. There are so many games that are played in life so we can't take everything so serious. Games are meant for fun. Enjoy every moment of the journey. God has a sense of humor, but he is not a man that should lie.

Don't spend your days here on earth living stressed out. How much time have you spent worrying about something that never came to pass? Imagine what you could have done with all of the valuable time. Worrying gets you nowhere. Too often we give power to stress and things that we can't control, causing us a world of problems. Don't focus on figuring out how things will work out; just believe that they will. Things often seem that they are not working out but they miraculously do or they work out as they should.

Fear is a scary giant to conquer. We were not born with the spirit of fear. That is learned behaviour. Does a child know danger or is that something taught by the parent's constant warnings of caution? We were born with the spirit to conquer fear. God created us to have powerful spirits, loads of love, and an impeccable mind to conquer fear. Be fearless.

I've said it before and I'll say it again, where you focus your energy is where the energy goes. You can focus on dreams and aspirations or you can focus on the adversities. We have the power of choice. We get to choose what we think about. We have the choice to train our minds just as we have the choice to train our bodies in the gym. Choose wisely. Choose not to rob your future from what is your right to happiness.

As you embark on your journey, don't be afraid to leave your mark. Let there be footprints left behind to show the traces of your journey. Leave behind a legacy that lives on long after you are gone. Step out on faith. Travel the world. Take chances. Explore what life has to offer. Don't leave this earth wishing you had lived to experience something. Live on purpose with purpose.

God gives me the direction and I have to praise him for it. I ask him to show me what's next and things happen. He provides opportunities and opens doors. "Show me thy ways, O Jehovah; Teach me thy paths" (Psalm 25:4). If I am not prepared to receive it, then the opportunity gets missed and is given to someone else or taken away. Life is filled with possibilities and opportunities. Be open to receive.

If I could sum up everything that my journey has taught me into key points for you to walk away with, it would be:

Thoughts become things

We attract more of what we focus on.

Earn your keep

Don't expect handouts. Every thing comes at a cost.

There are leaders and then there are followers

Every successful person in the world is a leader, but followers help build the dream because they can't handle the duties that come with being a leader. Both are important roles. Some people prefer the co-dependent.

Be passionate about your position.

Passion serves you, drives you, and shapes you. Whether you are an artist or a CEO, be passionate about it.

Seek motivation daily.

Food is the body's fuel. Motivation is the mind's fuel.

Have purpose

Don't be a leaf blowing in the wind. Whatever your purpose is, use it to advance your goals. Your purpose gives you direction.

Not everything is what it seems

Don't believe everything you hear and only half of what you see.

Be proactive not reactive

Take initiative and seize every opportunity. Be driven by your goals and not pulled by your fears.

Expect the best, but prepare for the worst

Always have a plan as your blueprint, but know that things will not always turn out the way we expect. Disappointments and surprises happen all the time.

Small circle, no squares

You do not need a lot of people around; you just need a good handful. Successful people are not surrounded by "YES" men/women. Choose your friends wisely.

Practice what you preach

Be an example. Live your motto. Living life the opposite of what you speak will turn those that look up to you into those who look down at you.

Conclusion

I encourage you to think about my story and what tools you can take away and add to your toolbox. It is time to take control of your life and live it the way it was intended to be lived. Stop living on autopilot and kick things into gear. The life you are meant to live is waiting for you to take the first/next step. I've given you A Walk in My Stilettos. I can talk the talk because I have walked the walk. I practice what I preach, and I am a living testimony to what a strong mind can do. "And now I stand here to be judged for the hope of the promise made of God unto our fathers" (Acts 26:6).

I've aspired to show you that despite struggle you can come out on top. How you react to the adversity will determine your future. Every choice you make will impact what direction your journey goes. For every action comes a reaction. Keep your eye on the prize and stay focused. I encourage you to share my story with your family, friends, and colleagues. Buy them a copy as a gift, and share the wealth of knowledge you just inherited.

There is so much power inside of you, inside of us all. Our strength comes from within. Fill your mind with images of abundance and happiness, and you shall never lack but have a storehouse stacked as great as you can imagine. Remember, you were born royalty. Keep your head high and stand tall in your own shoes. Stand on your story. Don't let your crown slip. Your steps have been divinely ordered!

About the Author

Makini Smith is an entrepreneur, a mother, mentor, an author and a leader in her community.

To her clients, Makini Smith is a trusted advisor for real estate that has received awards such as top producer starting from her first year; she is a pillar of strength and perseverance to her mentees. To her peers, Makini is highly regarded as an integrity-powered professional that knows how to make things happen in every area she tackles. She has been featured on numerous platforms for her wealth of knowledge and life experiences including teen motherhood, divorce, relationships, single parenthood, entrepreneurship and more.

"Give thanks by giving" is a motto that motivates her philanthropic contributions consistently. Inspiring women to strive for goals and become valuable members in the community to improve the lives of themselves and others is her passion. She enjoys bringing awareness to local charities and fundraising events. Makini was voted as 1 of 100 Black Women to Watch in Canada. Black Canadian Awards also honored her on their national wall of role models. The Canadian REALTORS Care Foundation has also recognized her outstanding community work.

Makini has graduated from the SisterTalk Circle Leadership Program designed for women leaders who would like to help other women live a more empowered & elevated life. She is a facilitator of the monthly meet ups. The program has given her the tools to mentor women that want to take their life to the next level.

Her obsession with shoes was the inspiration for the theme of her first published book "A Walk in My Stilettos: How to Get Through the Struggle with Grace" her journey of trials to triumph. Look out for more books to come in the "A Walk in My Stilettos" series.
Connect with the author on line at

Website: www.awalkinmystilettos.com
Email: info@awalkinmystilettos.com
Instagram: www.instagram.com/awalkinmystilettos
Facebook: www.facebook.com/awalkinmystilettos

MERAKI HOUSE

P U B L I S H I N G

Publishing with
Soul, Creativity & Love

Meraki House Publishing, founded in 2015 has established its brand as an independent virtual publishing house designed to suit your needs as the Author, delivering the highest quality design, writing and editorial, publishing and marketing services to ensure your success.

"Where your needs as an Author have become ours as an independent Publishing House."

WWW.MERAKIHOUSE.COM

In partnership with
www.designisreborn.com

Marnie Kay, Founder & CEO
marniekay.com

9 780994 961327